SELLING PILATES

Ron Thatcher

Order this book online at www.trafford.com/07-2035
or email orders@trafford.com

Most Trafford titles are also available at major online book retailers.

Note for Librarians: A cataloguing record for this book is available from Library and Archives Canada at www.collectionscanada.ca/amicus/index-e.html

Printed in Victoria, BC, Canada.

ISBN: 978-1-4251-4742-6

www.trafford.com

North America & international
toll-free: 1 888 232 4444 (USA & Canada)
phone: 250 383 6864 ♦ fax: 250 383 6804
email: info@trafford.com

The United Kingdom & Europe
phone: +44 (0)1865 722 113 ♦ local rate: 0845 230 9601
facsimile: +44 (0)1865 722 868 ♦ email: info.uk@trafford.com

10 9 8 7 6 5 4 3 2 1

This book is dedicated to:

Four little angels who have sacrificed
so I could follow my dreams.

The people who sacrificed in Indonesia
to make this book a reality.

Eddie Djauhari for all the hard work on the cover.

CONTENTS

Chapter 1 Introduction 1
Chapter 2 History of Pilates 4
Chapter 3 The Doctor 10
Chapter 4 How the System Works 16
Chapter 5 Pilates instructor Planner 19
Chapter 6 The Language of Sales 33
Chapter 7 How to Speak to a Guest 35
Chapter 8 The pilates Orientation 42
Chapter 9 The Quick Results Workout Card 46
Chapter 10 My Pilates presentation 48
Chapter 11 My Pilates script 53
Chapter 12 Introduction to the prescriptive presentation 56
Chapter 13 The Six Steps to a Professionally Structured Pilates training Program 58
Chapter 14 Price Presentation 60
Chapter 15 The Fisherman 63
Chapter 16 How and When to ***T.O.*** *67*
Chapter 17 Filling Out the Pilates Agreement 70
Chapter 18 How to Overcome Objections 75
Chapter 19 Closing
Chapter 20 My first experience as an instructor and the Ron Fletcher story 106
Chapter 21 The way to make your potential Clients know that they don't know 120
Chapter 22 Time Management 126
Chapter 23 Pilates Training Re-signs 129

Chapter 24 Master Appointment Book 132
Chapter 25 Working the Floor.. 135
Chapter 26 The wall of fame.. 138
Chapter 27 The Closeout Master Plan 141
Chapter 28 Selling Supplementation 147
Chapter 29 Interacting with staff 150
Chapter 30 Giving a free Gift with Purchase.......................... 156
Chapter 31 Confirming Appointments and cancellations 158
Chapter 32 Drilling 161
Chapter 33 To sell or not to sell 166

Chapter 1

INTRODUCTION

Welcome to ***Selling Pilates!!!*** This book is going to offer the Pilates instructor or fitness professional an amazing opportunity to understand and master the business side of Pilates. If you are ready to stop struggling and start producing, then get ready to enjoy the first book that has ever been written using the actual techniques coveted by the top Pilates instructors in the fitness industry.

This book will introduce you to the techniques that have built some of the largest, most successful training programs throughout the world. The fitness industry's top producers have kept these proven techniques secret for decades. The material contained within this book has been tested, tried and retested before being implemented to produce outstanding financial success. Not only will you get the inside track on how to get the most out of a career as a certified Pilates instructor, but you will also learn that establishing and maintaining a quality client list is a crucial aspect of your long-term success.

One unavoidable aspect of helping people to get results is collecting money; that is, if you are unable to sell your service, is it likely that you will be able to continue to give it away? I mean, what are you going to say the next time the studio owner asks you, "How many Pilates packages did you sell last month?" or "How many clients do you have resigning this week?" These are tough issues that nobody wants to write about or face up to. Let's be honest and to the point. **Selling is hard!** It is much easier to just not ask.

The bottom line is that it is much easier if you have been properly trained on how and when to propose the sale of a Pilates package. The anxiety that you are experiencing over asking for money will start to subside after reading this book. I know what you are thinking, "I am a Pilates instructor, not a salesman." Well, I have thought about this a lot and the simple fact of the matter is that you are a counselor, teacher, motivator, coach and sometimes even psychiatrist, but you are a salesman. However, not all Pilates instructors are working for commission, some are actually paid an hourly rate. If you are one of the "fortunate" ones working for a base salary, I am quite certain that it isn't very substantial.

A famous Chinese art teacher uttered the words
"the hard won work of the masters was not to be thrown away,
it was something to be challenged and emulated."

Operationally, your first days working as a Pilates instructor will consist of many long hours of self-education in relation to product knowledge. Sooner or later, you will begin to feel the pressure of the person who is in charge of driving revenue for your particular facility. Whether it's the stress from receiving small paychecks, or the pressure from the person in charge of production in your studio, you will feel that it is time to learn how to produce an income from your efforts. Your routine will no doubt start where most Pilates careers start and you will find yourself taking new clients through an orientation workout. Even if your studio does not offer this type of opportunity and you are responsible for creating your own sales opportunities, the fact remains the same. The best way to consistently produce new clients is to offer some sort of orientation or free introductory program. Success as a Pilates instructor is a derivative of converting these introductory "one time" workouts into long-term one-on-one Pilates clients. If you study the scripts, practicing methods and closing techniques in this book you will have more success than you ever dreamed possible. Soon, the road to financial success as a Pilates instructor will become clear and more enjoyable.

As an active Pilates studio operator, I find that I spend a good portion of my time trying to improve the fitness business as a whole. In recent times the Pilates studio industry has been criticized for using questionable business practices. This criticism always seems to center around the shortcomings of the selling process. In my opinion, the focus of this criticism should not be on the selling process. The shortcomings that I have recognized stem from the rapid growth of the fitness industry as a whole. This, coupled with a lack of systematic education, as well as the lack of long term employment opportunities are the true issues that plague the fitness industry. I have set out not only to increase investor support but also to improve and standardize training. I have tried to develop a process from which studio owners, managers and employees can systematically develop a long-term healthy plan for investors, clients and communities. My systems, like the ones used in my first book ***Fitness Memberships and Money*** are meant to be internalized so they can be practiced and utilized although they should merely act as a foundation upon which one should build and improve according to individual needs. I wrote this book with that philosophy in mind. I wrote this book for all the Pilates instructors that fear going to work at a job they love because they have to sell. I wrote this book to compensate for the certification programs that are misleading young students in regards to the day-to-day life as a Pilates instructor. I wrote this book for all the clients that say thank you for changing my life. Thank you for convincing me to make a decision today.

Chapter 2

HISTORY OF PILATES

"I must be right. Never an aspirin. Never injured a day in my life. The whole country, the whole world, should be doing my exercises. They'd be happier." - Joseph Hubertus Pilates, in 1965, age 86.

Engineered and built for commercial fitness, perfect for home use

I am sure most of you are familiar with the history of Joseph Pilates. For all accounts he is considered the founder of the equipment and philosophy. For those of you who are not familiar with the background this will be a brief summary.

Pilates was invented almost a hundred years ago by Joseph Pilates. Born in Germany in 1880, Pilates was by most accounts a sickly child who suffered from asthma, rickets and rheumatic fever. He was determined to overcome his health problems and he began to study anatomy and both Eastern and Western forms of exercise (including yoga, Zen, and ancient Greek and Roman regimens). By age 14 he transformed himself into a successful boxer, gymnast, skier and diver.

Joe went to England in 1912, where he worked as a self-defense instructor for detectives at Scotland Yard. There have even been accounts that he was a star circus performer. At the outbreak of World

War I, Joe was interned on the Isle of Man as an "enemy alien" with other German nationals. During his internment, Joe refined his ideas and trained other internees in his system of exercise. He became a nurse/caretaker to the many internees struck with wartime disease and physical injury. He began to devise equipment to rehabilitate them by taking bed springs and attaching them to the ceiling so even the bedridden could still stay strong. He rigged springs to hospital beds, enabling bedridden patients to exercise against resistance, an innovation that led to his later equipment designs.

Around 1914, Pilates was placed under forced internment along with other German nationals in Lancaster, England. There he taught fellow camp members the concepts and exercises developed over 20 years of self-study and apprenticeship in yoga, Zen, and ancient Greek and Roman physical regimens. It was at this time that he began devising the system of original exercises known today as "mat work", or exercises done on the floor. An influenza epidemic struck England in 1918, killing thousands of people, but not a single one of Joe's trainees died. This, he claimed, testified to the effectiveness of his system.

After his release, Joe returned to Germany. His exercise method gained favor in the dance community, primarily through Rudolf von Laban, who created the form of dance notation most widely used today. Hanya Holm adopted many of Joe's exercises for her modern dance curriculum, and they are still part of the "Holm Technique." When German officials asked Joe to teach his fitness system to the army, he decided to leave Germany for good.

Joseph Pilates called his method Contrology, which refers to the way the method encourages the use of the mind to control the muscles. Joseph Pilates preferred fewer, more precise movements, requiring control and form. He believed that mental and physical health were essential to one another and created what is claimed to be a method of total body conditioning that emphasizes proper alignment, centering, concentration, control, precision, breathing, and flowing movement, "The Pilates Principles." The program focuses on the core postural muscles that help keep the body balanced and are essential to providing support for the spine. In particular, Pilate's exercises teach awareness of breath and alignment of the spine, and strengthen the deep torso muscles, which are important to help alleviate and prevent back pain

Practiced faithfully, Pilates yields numerous benefits. Increased lung capacity and circulation through deep, healthy breathing is a primary focus. Strength and flexibility, particularly of the abdomen and back muscles, coordination-both muscular and mental, are key components in an effective Pilate's program.

Pilates, the theory, had gained notoriety prior to Joe's arrival and moved to the United States with an unknown practitioner. The first Pilates studio opened in New York City sometime around the year 1920. In 1926, Joe immigrated to the United States. During the voyage he met Clara, whom he later married. Joe and Clara opened a fitness studio in New York, sharing an address with the New York City Ballet. By the early 1960s, Joe and Clara could count among their clients many New York dancers. George Balanchine studied "at Joe's," as he called it, and also invited Pilates to instruct his young ballerinas at the New York City Ballet.

"Pilates" was becoming popular outside of New York as well. As the New York Herald Tribune noted in 1964, "in dance classes around the United States, hundreds of young students limber up daily with an exercise they know as a Pilates, without knowing that the word has a capital P, and a living, right-breathing namesake."

While Joe was the outspoken force behind his method, his wife Clara, a trained nurse, quietly incorporated his concepts and exercises in ways that benefited more seriously ill or injured clients. Her approachable style and special techniques spawned a dedicated lineage of teachers whose work flows through and uniquely colors the landscape of the Pilates method today. It is perhaps because of Clara that Pilates is clearly recognized as a positive form of movement-based exercise that truly can be tailored to any level of not just fitness, but also of health. The dance world caught on to the incredible effects of Pilates exercise regime and many of the greats such as Martha Graham, Jerome Robbins and George Balanchine incorporated Pilates principles into their lessons.

His students began to teach while Joe was still alive; only two of his students, Carola Trier and Bob Seed, are known to have opened their own studios. Trier, who had an extensive dance background, found her way to the United States by becoming a performing contortionist, after fleeing a Nazi holding camp in France. She found Joe Pilates in 1940, when a non-stage injury pre-empted her performing career. Joe Pilates assisted Trier in opening her own studio in the late 1950s. Joe and Clara remained close friends with Trier until their deaths.

Bob Seed was another story. A former hockey player turned "Pilates" enthusiast, Seed opened a studio across town from Joe and tried to take away some of Joe's clients by opening very early in the morning. According to John Steel, one day Joe visited Seed with a gun and warned Seed to get out of town. Seed went.

The second generation started teaching as well. Joe continued to train clients at his studio until his death in 1967, at the age of 87. When Joe passed away in 1967, he left no will and had designated no line of succession for the "Pilates" work to carry on. Nevertheless, his work would remain. Clara continued to operate what was known as the "Pilates" Studio on Eighth Avenue in New York, where Romana Kryzanowska became the director around 1970. Kryzanowska had studied with Joe and Clara in the early 1940s and then, after a 15-year hiatus spent in Peru, returned to renew her studies.

Several students of Joe and Clara went on to open their own studios. Ron Fletcher was a Martha Graham dancer who studied and consulted with Joe from the 1940s on. Fletcher opened his studio in Los Angeles in 1970 and attracted many Hollywood stars. Clara was particularly enamored with Ron and she gave her blessing to him to carry on the "Pilates" work and name. Like Carola Trier, Fletcher brought some innovations and advancements to the "Pilates" work. His evolving variations on "Pilates" were inspired both by his years as a Martha Graham dancer and by another mentor, Yeichi Imura.

Kathy Grant and Lolita San Miguel were also students of Joe and Clara who became teachers. Grant took over the direction at the Bendel's studio in 1972, while San Miguel went on to teach Pilates at Ballet Concierto de Puerto Rico in San Juan, Puerto Rico. In 1967, just before Joe's death, both Grant and San Miguel were awarded degrees by the State University of New York to teach "Pilates." These two are believed to be the only "Pilates" practitioners ever certified officially by Joe.

Other students of Joe and Clara who opened their own studios include Eve Gentry, Bruce King, Mary Bowen and Robert Fitzgerald. Eve Gentry, a dancer who taught at the Pilates Studio in New York from 1938 through 1968, also taught "Pilates" in the early 1960s at New York University's Theater Department. After leaving New York, she opened her own studio in Santa Fe, New Mexico. A charter faculty member of the High School for the Performing Arts, Gentry was also a co-founder of the Dance Notation Bureau. In 1979, she was given the "Pioneer of Modern Dance Award" by Bennington College.

In the 1970s, Hollywood celebrities discovered Pilates via Ron Fletcher's studio in Beverly Hills. Where the stars go, the media follows. In the late 1980s, the media began to cover Pilates extensively. The public took note, and the Pilates business boomed. "I'm fifty years ahead of my time," Joe once claimed. He was right. No longer the workout of the elite, Pilates has entered the fitness mainstream. Today, over 12 million Americans practice Pilates, and the numbers continue to grow.

Your first week as salesperson, you should try a game I invented. For one week answer every question asked with a question. This will help you understand the fundamentals of sales! Ron Thatcher

Chapter 3

THE DOCTOR

The mind is everything; what you think, you become. -Buddha

Alvin Stein III had spent much of his life studying to be a doctor. He had devoted his youth learning about the complicated and diverse systems of the human body, and he learned all the technical terms that were important in practicing medicine. Alvin's father and grandfather were both doctors. His father taught him well, ensuring that his son learned everything required of an upcoming successful physician. His father always taught him "that we don't heal books, we heal people," this would become more prevalent in the future.

Alvin was encouraged to become involved in sports and became a good all-around athlete at a young age. He was on the swimming team and the basketball team, earning an award for being the most improved swimmer in his senior year. Alvin received a partial scholarship as a student athlete and he was off to Stanford to begin his college education. He was excited about going to college, especially as he was going to an even more prestigious school than that of his father. He was very enthusiastic about becoming a medical doctor and was excited by the thought of saving a person's life. He was a diligent and hard working student who had joined the swimming team as a requirement of his scholarship, and had gone on to become a letterman with the Varsity Swimming Team. His college years passed quickly and he was soon applying for medical school.

His participation in athletics helped him mentally and emotionally in areas that left his peers challenged and at times struggling. Understanding the theory was an easy task for some of them, however attempting to utilize and demonstrate their knowledge in a practical manner was often too difficult. Many of the med-students failed to apply this knowledge and information while working on a cadaver. Alvin reflected on what his dad had once said and stated, "My dad was right! We don't heal books; many of the things that we learned in our books are actually very different once you study the anatomy of the human body." As medical school came to an end, Alvin was given the opportunity to complete his internship in Minnesota at the prestigious Mayo Clinic. Things were going well and the time for Alvin to actually commence his medical career was just around the corner.

Alvin moved away from his home in sunny California to complete his studies as an intern. Life was vastly different in Minnesota and he had a difficult time adjusting to the cold weather and the grueling 24-hour shifts. He also had his first feelings of self-doubt in this challenging environment filled with sickness and death. Alvin questioned whether he was capable of achieving his goal of becoming a doctor and called his father weekly for moral support and advice. He informed him of his difficulties and asked him if his internship experience had been similar.

Alvin's father offered understanding and encouraged him to be strong, "I completed my internship during a tour in the Vietnam War and it was atrocious. When I came back, being a doctor and running my own clinic was a breeze." He also reminded his son that the internship was designed to be a test. Once the test was over his life of being a doctor would be a breeze as well. Alvin had always wanted to learn the ropes from his dedicated dad. He soon completed his internship and was ready to start working in his father's busy clinic.

Alvin was doing well and business was thriving. However, soon after a distressing problem arose. The insurance companies were changing their policies, leaving older patients with insufficient coverage for adequate health care. Matters worsened when an elderly patient that Alvin had been treating passed away leaving his widow with medical bills and rejected insurance. This was starting to put serious pressure on the business and on Alvin's life. He began dreading work and the day soon came when he had to tell his father that he was going to leave the medical field.

His father said, "Son, I have been waiting for this day to come. I had hoped it wouldn't, but the day is here. I have something special for you. Your grandfather said this was an area of weakness in his profession. You see your grandfather was a genuine-hearted man and back in those days people were poor. They would die because they couldn't afford to pay the doctor. Your grandfather gave away so much free medical care that he himself went bankrupt. This book was given to your grandfather and it was an instrumental part of his ability to recover from financial ruin. It was given to your grandfather from a teacher at Harvard. The book was never published and it was really made up from secret techniques used by Harvard doctors who had run very successful clinics.

The book mainly focused on a different side of being a doctor. The cover of the book had only two words on it simply reading, 'Selling Medicine.' The book was not only given to your grandfather but it was also given to another doctor who was in your same situation. He was a talented doctor who had an incredible ability to cure the sick and was ready to give up.

This book has a reputation for being the savior of many generations of doctors." As Alvin's father pulled the book from an old dusty box, he explained that he searched high and low to retrieve the book because he knew that it had meant so much to his father. "I also knew that someday it just might come in handy. Now my son, I give the book to you. May you let the age-old words encompass the art of being a master of our trade. We must thank the hard-won work of those who have come before us, while also challenging and emulating their success in all areas." As Alvin opened the book, he noticed the penciled in writing. "My son this is a true story and it is to remind you that every case is as different in nature as the ailment from which it has come, some times the heart is the only medicine needed."

I am not talking about the patients; this book is to heal the Doctor!

"A Red Cross soldier"

One day, a Red Cross soldier who was selling anything in his bag from door to door to pay his way back over the border, found he had only one thin dime left. You see his plane had crash-landed during a peace mission, and he was very hungry.

He decided he would ask for a meal at the next house. However, he lost his nerve when a lovely young woman opened the door. Instead of a meal, he asked for a drink of water.

She thought he looked hungry, so she brought him a large bowl of soup. He ate it slowly, and then asked, "How much do I owe you?"

"You don't owe me anything," she replied. "Mother has taught us never to accept pay for a kindness."

He said, "Then I thank you from my heart."

As Alvin Stein left that house, he not only felt stronger physically, but his faith in man was stronger. He had been ready to give up and quit. Many years later, that same young woman became critically ill.

The local doctors were baffled. They finally sent her to the big city, where they called in specialists to study her rare disease. Dr. Alvin

Stein was called in for the consultation. When he heard the name of the town she came from, a strange light filled his eyes. Immediately, he rose and went down the hall to her room.

Dressed in his doctor's gown, he went in to see her. He recognized her at once. He went back to the consultation room and was determined to do his best to save her life. From that day, he gave special attention to her case. After a long struggle, the battle was won.

Dr. Stein requested the business office to pass the final bill to him for approval. He looked at it, and then wrote something on the edge and the bill was sent to her room. She feared to open it, for she was sure it would take the rest of her life to pay this bill.

Finally she looked, and something caught her attention on the side of the bill. She then read these words...

"Paid in full with one bowl of soup"

(Signed) Dr. Alvin Stein.

Tears of joy flooded her eyes as her happy heart prayed: "Thank You, God, that your love has spread broad through human hearts and hands."

You should remember this story my son! This book was given to me from a friend to help me cope with my own personal fear of dealing with the business side of being a doctor. You must trust your heart and remember not every case is the same.

Your father,

Alvin Stein the first

This was written in pencil by his own hand in the front of your Grandfathers book!

"Dad, are you saying that he gave this book to you?" "You were the doctor that was ready to give up, and Grandpa gave the book to you?" "WHAT IS THE BOOK REALLY ABOUT?" "It will teach you how to ask for money and make a living as a doctor!"

"My son, there are three different kinds of doctors in this world; the first are the ones that own clinics, they are good businessmen and they make the most money. The second are the doctors that work for the hospitals, they are the ones that don't like dealing with the business side so they let the hospitals deal with most of it, but they still get some of the patients coming back to them. The third is the doctor like the ones that do research and teach at schools, they hate the business side so much that they didn't even talk about *it* for the entire 12 years that they had spent at medical school. The business end of being a doctor brings out their worst fears and most of them were never willing to face those fears head on by taking up the challenge. Son, in all jobs there will be some parts that you may not like!"

"SOME PEOPLE WILL FOLD UP TENT AND QUIT,
THE STEINS FOCUS!"

Chapter 4

HOW THE SYSTEM WORKS

The system operates through constant repetition. It relies on systematic improvement of skills through practice. The system works with proven techniques to be used and referenced. Different areas of your arsenal must be used over and over in "real life" (role playing) situations until they are perfected. The system must be used and not merely read. When teaching systems, I get my staff to practice role-playing situations as opposed to me standing up and talking to them. This way I can be certain that they have learned the material, that they know how to use the scripts and that they are ready to deal with clients. I then make them present the material in front of a large group or the staff. If they can perform in front of the entire sales team, they can present it to a client or several guests.

If you are a manager and you want to know the key to success?
Inspect everything you expect!

I also make the staff accountable to have the scripts memorized by a certain date. If they do not have them memorized, then I make them present it to me every day until they do. Remember, the accountability factor is the key to managing the Pilates studio and yourself simultaneously. Nothing will be accomplished without accountability. If you are a self-starter this may be easy for you. If you are not, this task may take a little more time. You have to turn any system that you use in the Pilates studio into a habit. Once something is a habit, it becomes easier, enabling you to enjoy it more. The goals you set for yourself must be as important as the ones you set for your clients. You must approach them in the same manner: one step at a time.

If you are a new Pilates instructor the first thing you must do is memorize the sale presentation scripts word for word.

When small business Pilates studios transformed into big business, investors desired standardized systems. This is when I came into the picture. I worked for one of the largest Pilates studio companies in California. We had just reached the 20-studio milestone and we had received a large injection of cash to expand our company even further. Pilates had just become something that was offered to our clients and I had the unique opportunity to work in a studio that had been allocated for the pilot program. A pilot program is where you take a new system and you test it and try it in one particular location. Once you have taken a core system and developed it into something that works, you then work out the bugs and problems and finally you implement your system into the rest of the organization. Programs like these are developed with very careful planning and implemented under the watchful supervision of company management. The teams chosen for this difficult task were handpicked to deliver optimum results. As the systems for selling Pilates were developed, I had the opportunity to work as a Pilates counselor and was able to help bring this incredible new program to the front lines. We were a fantastic group of highly motivated individuals. We had drunk the potion and bought into the company systems, 110%. We believed that we were part of something that was going to change the industry and that we could make a difference in the lives of our Pilates clients. The system that we created took several months to complete and underwent many transformations before it became the product that most Pilates studio companies use today. Thousands of people have benefited from the results and the systems that were created during this pilot program. It is amazing the kind of energy you can create from a group of individuals that believe, and work toward achieving a common goal. I believe that my ability to build successful teams has come from my ability to duplicate this atmosphere in all the studios that I operate. Having one or two extraordinarily talented individuals can never compare with having a group of untalented, hardworking, system-believing people focused on one common success story. I feel that of all the Pilates systems that I have seen in the 35 studios that I have managed, this system has topped them all!

Soon after this program was developed, there was another large acquisition in California. The two largest Pilates studio companies merged and tried to combine their systems, leaving behind some of the secrets that built these wonderful organizations. I have had the privilege to see both systems at work in studios all over the world. Chicago to Nevada, California to China! The words and systems used in this book will unmistakably and without a doubt improve your ability to sell Pilates.

Chapter 5

PILATES INSTRUCTOR PLANNER

Training materials should be kept in the front of your planner and should be referenced as often as possible or whenever needed. As discussed in Chapter 4, I prefer my instructors to memorize various scripts for different situations. Memorizing these various scripts is the first thing a new Pilates instructor should do. If you are unable to memorize the ten or so pages of script, you should do nothing else until you perfect that area of your arsenal.

If you are not able to perform an effective orientation appointment, and if you do not know how to present Pilates or how to set up a take over (TO), then you should practice in these areas before taking any guests. Once these scripts are memorized, such as the introduction, then these training materials will be used as a reference and training tool. It sounds like a lot of work, but believe me it makes the job easier and more profitable.

Once a month you should train in each area of the book. If you do this, your sales skills will remain sharp and you will have the ability to learn and grow. Remember the fitness industry is a rapidly growing business and change is essential for continued growth and improvement. If certain areas of the training process are not working or you are not improving, then you, as a professional, have to improve the training information you are using.

If you fail to plan, you plan to fail

To-Do List

I found that the personal to-do list is a simple and effective tool that has been used for years by everyone from the common housewife to the President of the United States. It is a simple concept. When you think of something that is important, write it down! This will put it on your priority list, limiting mistakes and leaving your mind free to think of other things. You can cross off each task as you accomplish it and remaining items can be circled and transferred to the next day's to-do list. This can be an effective habit. I find that people who use this simple tool are more efficient, make fewer mistakes, and get more accomplished. Although this is your business planner, personal matters can still be taken care of at work. It is okay to list personal matters on your to-do list.

Goals and Projections

Goals and projections should be updated daily. This is the most functional way of learning how your production can influence your numbers. As the old saying goes, "the numbers do not lie." This is especially true in our business. The numbers tell us what we are doing right and what we are doing wrong. The numbers are our guides to success. They will show you what happens when you have a bad day, and they will show you what happens when you have a good day. Most importantly, they will show you what happens when you are not set up for that day.

My definition of a successful person is a person that can set goals and then achieve those goals.

What happens to your paycheck when you hit your goals? I bet you can answer that question for yourself. Having an organized "Goals and Projections" section in your planner will show you what you have to do daily; it gives you the ability to control your numbers more consistently and will offer you a daily affirmation of your goals. I prefer to track every area of sales separately. Within each area, I have five steps:

Gross Sales: goal, last day worked, month to date, projection and percentage

EFT: goal, last day worked, month to date, projection and percentage

Pilates: goal, last day worked, month to date, projection and percentage

Supplements: goal, last day worked, month to date, projection and percentage

Retail: goal, last day worked, month to date, projection and percentage

Other goals: last day worked, month to date, projection and percentage

If kept updated consistently and correctly, these areas will keep us more organized and help increase our sales. We begin by setting goals and then use our materials to project our progress as we go along. Each month you should set goals based on the previous month's performance. Like most successful salespeople, your sales goal should increase each month, as your ability to hit these goals increases. As you hone your sales skills, your comfort level and confidence increase enabling you to achieve higher goals. I personally never set goals that are too easy to achieve. At the same time, I never set goals that are impossible to achieve. You want the goal to be lofty enough to motivate you but not so high that you cannot achieve it. The goal should be in line with what you want your paycheck to be. If you set a goal that is $200,000 in sales and your commission is 10 percent, you will earn $20,000 commission before taxes; therefore, you cannot expect to bring home a $30,000 paycheck! The first goal that should be set is what you want your income to be. Based on that, you can calculate how much you need to sell. You now have your goal.

For Example:

Your desired income is \$50,000	50,000
Your commission from each sale is 10%	x10
You must sell	\$500,000

Being able to meet your goals will make you a highly effective Pilates instructor and you will be able to control your financial destiny. The sky is the limit! The last day worked column is what you sold the last day in each area. The month to date column is a running total; it represents the updated total amount you have sold up to that date for the month. The projection column is the month to date divided by the days gone by, times the total days in the month. The percentage column is your projection divided by your goal.

For Example for Projection:

month to date divided by days gone by.

x

Total days in the month. = Projection

It is the second day of a 30-day month. Yesterday you sold \$2,000 in gross sales. Your month to date is \$2,000. One day has gone by, and so you divide 2000 by 1 times 30 days in the month. It means that the total amount you are projecting is \$60,000. Divide that by your goal of \$70,000. You are at 86 percent of your goal.

For example:

2,000 x 30

1 = 60,000 = 86%

70,000

You now have 29 days left in the month to reach your goal. Since you sold \$2,000 on the first day of the month, you now have only \$68,000 left to reach your goal. In order to find your daily goal you must subtract your month to date from your goal, then divide by how many days are left in the month. The numbers show that you must sell an average of \$2,344 per day for the rest of the month to achieve 100 percent of your original goal.

For example:

70,000 $\frac{68{,}000}{29}$ = **$2,344**

- 2,000

68,000

Updating your statistics is something that should be done every day. You should make this a strict habit and it should be the first thing you do every morning after you walk through the studio. The numbers, good or bad, will show you the areas that you have to focus on for that day. They also show the areas that you are doing well in and the areas that need improvement.

Finally, your daily appointment sheets will have areas for all important appointment information. Each day's sheet will have sections for logging the time of the appointment, for confirmation, the person's name, their work and home telephone number, a note about the appointment, and finally, the outcome.

Appointments

The **time** section stands for what time you are scheduling the appointment. You write the individual's information next to the time they are expected to arrive for their appointment. You should highlight certain areas of the day to be filled in by the front desk and/or the sales staff to ensure that your appointment book is filled with high quality orientations. The **confirmation** box will allow you to make a note if the appointment has been confirmed. In addition one should check the book regularly to see if any new appointments have been scheduled. It is also advisable to call and reconfirm prior to an appointment to save you from being inconvenienced, for example driving into work only to have to leave again. Finally, ensure that all of your clients are able to contact you at anytime with last minute cancellations. (Please see chapter 31, page 158, Confirming appointments and cancellations.)

PILATES
TRAINING
PLANNER
PILATES TRAINING PLANNER
CUSTOM MADE PLANNER
HOW TO MASTER THE BUSINESS SIDE
OF BEING THE ULTIMATE
PILATES TRAINER

Monthly Success Plan

(Name)__________ (Month)___________

GOAL

Gross_______ EFT_______ PT_______ Other_______

I will complete the steps below and hit my personal goals by the end of this month.

1、____

____

2、____

____

3、____

____

4、____

____

5、____

____

6、____

____

(Signature)_______________ (Date)______________

(Manager)________________ (Date)______________

MONTHLY CALENDAR

SUNDAY	MONDAY	TUESDAY	WEDNESDAY	THURSDAY	FRIDAY	SATURDAY
SUNDAY	MONDAY	TUESDAY	WEDNESDAY	THURSDAY	FRIDAY	SATURDAY
SUNDAY	MONDAY	TUESDAY	WEDNESDAY	THURSDAY	FRIDAY	SATURDAY
SUNDAY	MONDAY	TUESDAY	WEDNESDAY	THURSDAY	FRIDAY	SATURDAY
SUNDAY	MONDAY	TUESDAY	WEDNESDAY	THURSDAY	FRIDAY	SATURDAY
SUNDAY	MONDAY	TUESDAY	WEDNESDAY	THURSDAY	FRIDAY	SATURDAY

TODAY'S CLIENT APPOINTMENTS

TIME	SOURCE	CONF	NAME	PHONE #	RESULTS	TIME	SOURCE	CONF	NAME	PHONE #	RESULT
8AM						3PM					
:30						:30					
9AM						4PM					
:30						:30					
10AM						5PM					
:30						:30					
11AM						6PM					
:30						:30					
12PM						7PM					
:30						:30					
1PM						8PM					
:30						:30					
2PM						9PM					
:30						:30					

All missed guests should be given passes and have appointment on closeout

Missed Guest without Pass: Blue
MIssed Guest with Pass: Yellow
Enrolled Guest: Green
DI & NI: Orange

DAILY TO-DO LIST

- Walk through the studio. (Meet and greet clients and check equipment for maintenance and cleanliness.)
- Confirm Pilates appointments and orientations.
- Update your statistics and personal planner.
- Update and check the Master Training Appointment Book.
- Check and call all new clients agreements from the previous day and make orientation appointments and use welcome greetings.
- Schedule at least three orientation appointments.
- Sit in on three new clients presentations.
- Workout with one other Pilates instructor and compare techniques, role-play on sales presentations.
- Check-out with your Pilates supervisor and make sure your goals are achieved.

DAILY AFFIRMATION

Gross

/ / / / /

LDW MTD PROJ. % GOAL DAILY NEED

EFT

/ / / / /

LDW MTD PROJ. % GOAL DAILY NEED

Deals

/ / / / /

LDW MTD PROJ. % GOAL DAILY NEED

Pilates Training

/ / / / /

LDW MTD PROJ. % GOAL DAILY NEED

Supplements

/ / / / /

LDW MTD PROJ. % GOAL DAILY NEED

Pilates Payment Plan

Agreement #	Client Name	Instructor	Total Package Price	Payment Method	Date Payment 1	Date Payment 2	Date Payment 3	Potontial Resign Date

Pilates Tracking Sheet

Instructor Name:

Package Purchase Date:

Client Name:

Total Sessions:

Client Phone No.:

	Client's Name	Date of Session	Time of Session	Signature
1				
2				
3				
4				
5				
6				
7				
8				
9				
10				
11				
12				
13				
14				
15				
16				

QR1 QR2 Monthly Tracking Sheet QR1 QR2

Instructor: Month:

Client's Name	QR1 Date QR1	Client Signature	QR2 Date QR2	Client Signature	Pilates Client (Yes/No)

Meeting Notes

<u>All</u> notes taken at our club for any reason should be put in the notes section of your planner, if it is written anywhere else, it will get lost.

Chapter 6

THE LANGUAGE OF SALES

Rejection Words	**Acceptable Substitutes**
Contract	Pilates Agreement, Agreement, Paperwork, Form
Cost or Price	Investment or Amount
Down Payment	Initial Investment, Initial Amount, One-time Investment
Monthly Payment	Monthly Investment or Monthly Amount
Sell or Sold	Get involved or Get started
Deal	Package or Opportunity
Pay For	Take care of
Sign	Authorize, Approve, Endorse, OK it
Crowded	Popular, Exciting, Active Environment
Salesperson	Instructor, Pilates Instructor,
Dollars	Omit this word altogether—the only possible exception is when the guest is comparison shopping, and your studio is a better value because it will save him or her so many dollars per month or year
Commission	Fee for service
Objection	Concern
If	When
Cheap	Affordable
Diet	Nutritional Program, Food Intake
Pitch, Spiel.	Presentation
High Pressure	Enthusiasm, Concern, My passion
Prizewinner, "up" here	Guest, appointment
On a free pass or walk-in	
Sign up, join.	Get involved, get started

Victorious warriors win first and then go to war,
while defeated warriors go to war first and then seek to win.
-Suntzu

It is important to know that certain words can create an emotional response from your prospective Pilates client. It is important to practice and use only the words that are going to work in your favor.

For Example

"Mom I'm going to the Pilates studio to get a package" The mother responds, "Make sure you don't sign anything without reading it first and make sure you don't get involved in any contracts!"

People remember these little things. I don't know why but they just seem to pop up when we use certain words. So practice using the right words and your job will be a lot easier, just like second nature.

Chapter 7

HOW TO SPEAK TO A GUEST

Building instant rapport can come from something as simple as addressing a person by their first name.

A true sales professional and Pilates instructor understands the basic fundamentals when it comes to speaking to a potential client. Rapport and comfort levels with a client can be created or destroyed almost immediately.

It may sound redundant, but make certain to do the following:

1. Smile, use a firm handshake and maintain eye contact.
2. A proper greeting and introduction is essential. Be sure to introduce yourself and use the client's name.
3. Build rapport by asking many questions. A proper needs analysis can be the key to making the sale. Do not give up too much information before you truly understand your potential client's intentions. (Use your studios orientation card and perform a proper needs analysis.)
4. Be kind and courteous at all times and be sure to let your client do most of the talking. **(You have two ears and one mouth for a reason!)**
5. It is important to remain indirect when attempting to close the sale. You must develop the ability to maintain good rapport through five closing attempts. (This will only happen if you use the steps outlined in Chapter 16, How to Overcome Objections.)

Sales language

Only seven percent of all communication is verbal which is a fact that many people find hard to believe. Ninety-three percent of our communication has nothing to do with the words that you produce, but more so to do with the non-verbal communication that we use. Non-verbal communication consists of tone of voice, eye contact, facial expressions, and proximity to another person. All of these factors come into play when you're communicating with another individual. A sales person or Pilates instructor's inability to endear this concept can very easily limit their revenue production and personal income levels. Let's look at this scenario:

One instructor presents a Pilates package to a prospective client, but they do not purchase it. Another instructor steps in and performs a full transference of emotions into that prospective client and sells them a package while using the exact same words that the first instructor used. The reason why this happens is that you may be talking to your client, but you are not really *communicating* with them. A full transference of emotions is making your prospect feel what you are feeling, the passion for fitness and the need for proper education through a Pilates instructor!

There are different ways to communicate the same words, each providing a different meaning to the receiver. You can look at someone and smile, then laugh and call him or her a name. You can also scream in someone's face and call him or her a name. These are two vastly different forms of communication with totally different meanings. They will also achieve two totally different results. You have to be aware of how and what you are communicating. You must help your prospect to understand that you truly care and want to help them attain their personal goals. These are techniques that come naturally to some people and are often difficult to teach. It takes a lot of trial and error. Some people pick up the knack of communicating, or they may have learned naturally through their parents. The bottomline is that it is very important to pinpoint the communication style of your guest.

The true meaning of sales is the transference of emotions. Your prospect needs to truly feel and believe in what you are saying. You will come to the point where you learn how to manipulate through communication. This happens once you have memorized the scripts, inserted your personality into them, and effectively learned how to "mirror" your prospect. These certain forms of communication are less verbal than you may think. The first step in learning the sales process is verbal communication: saying the right words, asking the right questions, getting the person to agree by "using tie downs," all the things that can come across the desk verbally. The T.O. process will enable you to watch your manager and listen to other salespeople who may be better than or more experienced than you. You will begin to learn that there are other areas of communication such as the non-verbal. This form of communication creates the certain energy that flows across the desk and can't be heard. Have you ever shown a guest the prices and observed their face turning red? No doubt you start to sense the friction at the table even tough they haven't said a word. You can clearly see the non-verbal communication coming across the table, the red face and the moving in the seat. You can feel all of the emotions that your guest is projecting. That flow of energy coming across the desk is what I am talking about. A professional knows how to harness and control that energy and use it to close more packages.

Why do you get up from a sales presentation? What does it accomplish? Why do we do that? It clears the air of all the emotions that were flowing back and forth between you and the guest, and enables them to relax. One of your goals is to comfort your client, which can be achieved by helping them to loosen up and feel good about making a purchase. They can't do that if they feel the friction across the desk. There is no denying that people project energy and you should make sure that you are aware of this. Study this and know that it can hold you back from making sales.

You can say all the right things to a guest and everything may seem to be going well, but there is still something missing. What is it? They feel uncomfortable and uneasy about buying a package from *you*. You said all the right things and were nice to the person, but deep down inside the potential client felt that you weren't being honest or they felt that something just wasn't right. The greeting and introduction is an overlooked but vital aspect of our business. Many studio managers and Pilates instructors neglect to devise a uniform greeting strategy when faced with a prospective member.

Greeting and Introduction

This is an area that, when focused on correctly, will improve the relationship with the client, decrease tension and ultimately lead to an increase of sales. There are many different ways of doing this but remember that, "you never get a second chance to make a first impression." See the following script as an example of the method that I prefer to use in this situation.

"How are you?" (Wait for response)

"My name is John, and what is your name?" (Wait for response)

"Mr. '*Soon to be client*', what I would like to do is take a moment of your time to find out exactly what you are looking to accomplish Then I will ask you a couple of questions in regard to your current fitness level and goals in the facility. Finally when we are finished, I will take you through some basic exercises. Sound fair?" (Wait for response)

"Great."

Since I believe in a consistent system approach, I feel it is important to avoid making the introduction too complicated. Many instructors will not use a system approach for fear it will limit their personality and many employers fear that they may not be able to successfully teach it to new employees. They view it as more of a burden than it is worth, avoiding the implementation of a standard introduction and presentation, which can, in effect, be detrimental to sales.

Building Rapport

In order to consistently produce sales of any type, one must build rapport with a prospective client. Building good rapport allows you to build a comfort zone and a trust between yourself and the prospect. If there is no trust, there is no sale.

You must attempt to think as they would think and you must be patient and mindful of their questions and concerns. People rarely trust those they do not like or feel comfortable with. Being humble and kind in all situations will help to earn this trust.

Take a moment to think of the people you surround yourself with. I am going to guess that you probably trust and like the people that you call "friends". The most successful sales people in this business build mini-relationships with the majority of their prospects. Having good rapport means that you communicate well with another person, you are friendly, and you trust one another. If you think of each prospect as a potential friend, you will immediately find yourself more comfortable when speaking with them.

The easiest way to build a strong rapport with your prospect is by uncovering possible common interests that you may have. It is easy for a person to say "no" to a person they do not like, or a person they have nothing in common with.

Remember the **K-I-S-S** rule. It means **K**eep **I**t **S**imple **S**tupid! Even though you want to build rapport and find common interests, you want to do this in a simple, comfortable fashion. Be careful not to offer too much information about yourself before discovering what their interests are. Ask your prospect questions and find common interests based on their answers. Giving up too much information about yourself before you know the interests of your client can cause problems that are hard to overcome.

For example, John is attempting to sell a Pilates package to Tom. Tom explains that he is a huge football fan, he lives in the Bay Area, and football is his life. John replies that the Bay Area is a beautiful place, and he loves San Francisco. "Go 49ers!" Tom explains that he lives in Oakland, and he is a Raiders fan!

In this situation, the salesperson did not find out the proper information before speaking. The salesperson was too quick with his response and did not pre-qualify. Therefore, since Tom's life is football, now opposite interests have been established and John's sale is now increasingly more difficult. The salesperson/prospect relationship is one of give and take. You will find yourself in situations where you share no common interests with a prospect. In fact, you are not going to care in the least about some of their interests and quite often you will find yourself disagreeing with their opinions. These are the times when you must remember that you are a professional, not a fan, and you are the one who must stay in control. Always try to keep a smile on your face and keep after *your* goal.

Mirroring and Matching

Along with memorizing your scripts, you must learn to "mirror" your prospects. "Mirroring" allows one to build rapport by utilizing the same voice tones, facial expressions, and body language as the person they are engaging. We will always feel more comfortable with someone that we feel parity with. The most successful sales people in the world not only find common bonds verbally, but do so physically as well. This is a very vital and overlooked aspect of being a Pilates instructor and a salesperson. You **must** find common ground with your potential client as this can be the difference between gaining a new client and losing one. When used properly, mirroring means having the ability to change the way you act, talk, and the speed in which you react or walk in accordance with the prospective client. This is not something that I can outline for you. It is not something that is easy to teach. It is an effective tool that, when mastered, can make an unbelievable impact on your sales numbers and your income.

For Example:

If the prospect is shy, you cannot be aggressive. If you have a prospect that walks slowly, you cannot walk fast. If your prospect talks quietly, you need to talk quietly. If your prospect leans back and crosses their legs during your sales presentation, you need to do so as well. Get the picture?

This area of your arsenal can go much deeper. You have to be like a chameleon, a lizard that has the ability to change its color and shape to meet its surroundings.

Chapter 8

THE PILATES ORIENTATION

The Pilates orientation or complimentary workout has become a very important aspect of the Pilates sales process. As the Pilates sales process began to evolve, we found that the most difficult obstacle to overcome was getting the Pilates instructors to go out on the floor and take a client through a complimentary workout. It has proven to be difficult to get instructors to approach clients and offer their services. We felt that the key to a successful Pilates studio operation must lie in getting our clients results. We found that most of the members that dropped out of the studio were the ones that didn't see any results within the first 6 weeks. As a remedy to these two problems, we developed a program that would benefit instructors and members alike. It would give the instructors an opportunity to offer their services as well as giving every single member an opportunity to work with an instructor possessing the knowledge to set a successful program in motion. This program could show the benefits and the value of the one-on-one Pilates program. We truly felt that the success of the Pilates department and the Pilates studio would depend on producing quality opportunities for the instructors. We also felt that every individual who joined the studio should get a chance to experience some Pilates education. At that time, we made the decision that every person, whether they joined on a membership or were given a free pass to the studio, would receive three sessions with a Pilates instructor. At the end of the third session, they would be brought to the table and given a presentation or talk about how their orientation went. We would also find out what vitamins they needed and if they were interested in continuing with Pilates.

Expose yourself to various conditions and learn - *Bruce Lee*

Keep Them Coming

In order to be a successful instructor you must keep a consistent influx of new clients coming your way. There are several ways of doing this. One way is to be able to work the floor. The other way is to produce a great line of quality buddy referrals. The only problem with this is that they require a natural sales ability. We have found that many instructors were unable to use this system consistently. The best instructors in our business were the ones that had the ability to pick and choose clients based on consistent re-signing of clients, continued orientation sign ups, and a dedication toward reaching their goals.

If you maintain a consistent approach towards creating daily orientations you will be booked with quality Pilātes clients. The over sold clients can easily be passed down to other instructors in the studio that have fewer clients or may just be starting out. Pick and choose the clients you work well with. Build a relationship with other Pilates instructors, and allocate a system to send over bookings to these newer or less fortunate team members. Remember the more quality clients you train and maintain, the more you can charge for your service.

In review, every member who joined the studio was offered three free forty minute training sessions to orientate the members to the studio. The original program consisted of a three step process, the first #1, a questionnaire and a fitness assessment followed by a short test. The second, #2 session consisted of a brief cardio introduction and a split 50% body resistance workout. The third, #3 session consisted of the unused muscle from the previous day and a brief presentation of the benefits of other studio services and Pilates sessions.

The Orientation Card

I felt that the early orientation program worked well and produced great numbers. The program that I now recommend for best results has come from a modified system that has been tested, tried and improved. Your orientation cards or questionnaires will vary from studio to studio depending on your particular demographic. It is important to understand that your particular company has put a lot of time and effort into creating this service to the members.

I believe that if you have been properly trained and you do a quality orientation, you will find that in most cases your studio has created substantial value using their orientation card. Looking at the orientation program from an ownership stand point, most companies have determined that this program has substantial cost involved and many of the large Pilates studios chains have shortened this program to meet financial obligations. Whether your company offers one complimentary session or ongoing sessions, the fact remains the same. Offering free Pilates sessions and using your company's standardized goal sheet will improve your selling ability.

Here are some pointers:

- Schedule quality orientations making sure that you have several each and everyday, will improve your business.
- Book orientations for times that you have openings in your schedule. Most likely your potential clients will book their orientation at the same time they are interested in receiving the one-on-one Pilates Packages.
- It is important to use the communication skills outlined in Chapter 7 and to build rapport with your potential client. Even if the member is not interested in ongoing sessions, they are still very important to the studio and your first impression may be a lasting one.

- It is important to be informative, but equally important to ask questions, make notes and pay close attention to the education level of your potential client. Using technical information may overwhelm or invoke fear.
- It is important to spend some time on the written part of the interview, but it is also equally important to spend time building rapport and not focusing so much on the technical and the written parts of the interview. Spending more time understanding the person can be more important than the Pilates.
- Normally, as a rule of thumb, we do not present Pilates on the first orientation. In some cases, your potential client may show an interest in one-on-one sessions during your first interview. If this were the case, I would recommend doing a full presentation on the one-on-one sessions available.
- Depending on which presentation you like best, I would recommend learning it word for word until you are so comfortable that you can add your own personality and style. Once you have done this, your presentation should sound smooth and should not sound memorized.

Chapter 9

THE QUICK RESULTS WORKOUT CARD

Date:________________________ Q.R.1 Q.R.2
Guest Name:__________________ ______ ______
Instructor:____________________
Name:______________ Date of birth:__________Age:________
Address: ____
Phone:(H)_____________(O)_____________(HP)_____________
E-mail:________________________ Occupation:______________
Emergency Contact:______________________________________

Health Screening

Have you had or ever experienced:

- ❑ Dizziness or fainting?
- ❑ Any heart condition
- ❑ High(low)Blood pressure
- ❑ Stroke
- ❑ Diabetes
- ❑ Any pain or injury to the joints
- ❑ Pregnant or given birth in the past 1 yr
- ❑ Any major surgery
- ❑ Any other medical conditions that we should be aware of?

I am aware that physical exercise can subject me to serious injury and that if I engage in physical activity or use any Number One Pilates facility or participate in any Number One Pilates sponsored event I do so entirely at my own risk. I release Number One Pilates and its directors, officers, and agents from any liability to me or damage or loss to any of my personal property in connection with my use of Number One Pilates facilities or equipment or my participation in Number One Pilates sponsored activities. I understand that I am giving up legal rights that I might otherwise have and that this release includes without limitation, damages I may suffer as a result of (1) my use of any exercise equipment, product or Number One Pilates facility, (ii) the malfunctioning of any Number One Pilates equipment, (iii) any Number One Pilates instruction or supervision, and (iv) slipping, falling, or otherwise injuring myself in any manner while on the Number One Pilates premises, including sidewalks and parking areas.

Member Signature:________________________Date:____________

Pilates Fitness Goals

Please check on the goals you want to achieve in embarking on an exercise program:

- ❑ Improve flexibility
- ❑ Improve on a sport specific performance
- ❑ Sculpting and toning
- ❑ Improve coordination
- ❑ Increase strength
- ❑ Ability to cope with stress
- ❑ Increase lung capacity and circulation
- ❑ Increasing energy level
- ❑ Improve cardiovascular fitness
- ❑ Social

On the scale of 1-5, how would you rate your current fitness level?

(1, 2, 3, 4, 5)

Can you give a brief description of your current fitness activity for one week?

When was the last time that you felt that your fitness level met or exceeded acceptable levels?

Please list a brief description of an average nutrient intake over a two day period. Please include alcohol, coffee, cigarette, prescriptions or dietary vitamins.

What is the most convenient time for you to exercise, morning, afternoon or evening?

What is your current work or school schedule?

How much time would you be allocating towards accomplishing your Pilates goals?

Chapter 10

MY PILATES PRESENTATION

There are two ways to work. You can work hard or you can work smart. I found the latter to be much more lucrative.

This is the point where I am given the opportunity to reveal the presentation that really changed the face of Pilates fitness. For the majority of the instructors back in the days when these pilot programs were being developed, selling their service was the last thing on their mind. The Pilates instructor was just a guy or girl out on the floor that helped give some good pointers and maybe once in awhile, if you were lucky or good looking, you would get some rich old person to pay money to have you teach them how to do Pilates. Most of the instructors honestly believed that the service they provided was reserved only for a certain class! If I was to "stereo-type;" the average young, new Pilates instructor, they did not believe in their own self worth and to most young instructors 50 dollars for 1 hour of their training services was just an unheard of amount of money. So, we decided to make it our goal to find out where the shortcomings were in the Pilates area. Once we pinpointed what the shortcomings actually were, we set our goal and then we developed a plan of how we would overcome each of our obstacles. It may sound rather scientific but this was a business plan and we confronted it accordingly. We realized that the Pilates department could be one of the fastest growing revenue centers in our studios. We believed that we could set ourselves apart by offering the most successful program to our members. We truly believed that we could create a way of life that generated results. If we could teach our clients that by using Pilates sessions to develop good effective habits people from all walks of life would be able to enjoy the benefits of Pilates. A large percentage of top athletes, successful movie actors, and even executives have worked with professional instructors to achieve maximum results. We knew what the major key to our business was, always stay focused and remember that the main obstacle would be getting results. It was also important that we understand a successful system for learning how to sell Pilates. We believed that the first step in selling Pilates was to get potential clients in front of an instructor so that they would understand what it is that the instructors do. The second step is that you must understand the benefits of the Pilates program. The third step is to develop a presentation that builds the value of this extremely precious program. The fourth step is presenting the different price options and the fifth step is getting the commitment and closing the sale.

Step One: Understanding What It Is the Instructors Do

We believed that the instructors needed a benefits building program that would be so powerful that no closing was necessary; the following is what was created. The instructors also focus on other important areas such as those outlined below.

Goal setting for the client, setting achievable goals within a specific time frame and putting everything down on paper. This ensures that the client can track their improvement. The instructors also focus on other important areas such as those outlined below.

Food intake, working with the type of food that clients like to eat.

Accountability, ensuring that the members show up to their scheduled appointments.

Consistency, making sure that the member is working out on a consistent basis, about 3 to 4 times per week.

Motivation, is needed to consistently hit your goals and ensure that you get the most out of every single workout.

Proper Techniques to avoid injuries and to ensure the optimal benefit to the member.

Program Design, individualizing the program to achieve long-term results and a lifetime education of Pilates. Tie downs were added at the end of each step to gain minor agreement.

Step Two: The Benefits of Pilates

The benefits of Pilates are endless, and practiced faithfully, numerous. Increased lung capacity and circulation through deep, healthy breathing is a primary focus. Strength and flexibility, particularly of the abdomen and back muscles, coordination-both muscular and mental, are key components in an effective Pilates program.

A better, longer life through exercise; an education that will stay with you for the duration of your life; better self-esteem; a positive impact on your personal relationships; better performance at work; more energy; healthy meal planning; and lower stress levels. This is just a portion of the benefits. The possibilities are endless.

Step Three: The Presentation of Benefits

I personally recommend that you come up with a script that will build up the benefits and add value to your presentation. I used a script developed by one of the top Pilates instructors in our company at the time. Your script may resemble a script like this one (refer to chapter 11, page 53) or the one I recommended previously for the greeting and introduction. I worked with an outstanding instructor who lent his script to all the salespeople to help them increase Pilates sales. It was three pages long and it took me a month to memorize, but it worked great. The first month I used the presentation my sales went through the roof and I sold $9,000 in Pilates. It focuses on building the benefits of the training program and helps the clients to understand exactly what they are paying $50 an hour for. Remember, you cannot show a person in one hour precisely what it is the Pilates instructor is going to help them accomplish. Therefore, you have to paint a picture in the persons' mind of the benefits they are going to receive from this service. If the benefits outweigh the loss, your clients will be willing to make the trade, money for results.

Step Four: Price Presentation

You should have a price presentation that has several different options and programs. There should be a program to fit every budget from executives to students. The program should be able to meet the needs of all the individual goals. There are many different goals that the members will have. A few of the most common are weight loss, weight gain, rehabilitation, toning and firming programs, and a basic introduction to fitness. Your studio should have packages priced from $50 to $5,000 and sessions that range from one to fifty. These are the standard pricing ranges and sessions that most successful studios have. The presentations at your particular studio will vary so you should check with your fellow instructors to ensure consistency.

Step Five: Closing the Sale

Your prospective client will give you the exact same objections that you will get when you are trying to sell anything. You will hear everything from "I need to think about it" to "I need to talk it over with my husband". Your closing techniques should be the same as with a membership and you should include everything from "TO'ing" to "price dropping" to "post dated checks". You will even use commitment questions such as "If I could get you a good deal would you want to commit to achieving your Pilates goals today?" You have to realize that Pilates accounts for approximately 30% of the gross sales in fitness centers today. Your members in the studio are willing to spend their money and time because they are interested in achieving long-term results. Pilates is the most effective method the clients can rely on in order to achieve those results. This is a very important aspect of what we do and if you cannot master this area, you will never be a complete professional, and you will be left behind in our industry.

After you have finished your quick results session and before you show the price presentation. Make sure your client is sitting down and you have presented the 7 steps. You will want to make sure all the little questions are out of the way. You do not want to answer any questions when it comes time for you to show prices or during the price presentation. Before moving into your presentation, always ask, *"Is there any additional questions you may have before we go through the different package options?"* You may say, *"Other than the price options do you have any other question or concerns?"* You always want to use a printed price sheet or laminate because it will add credibility to your options.

Price presentations add creditability to your studio. If you pull out a piece of paper and a pen, it shows your packages are open for negotiation. Your guest will be more likely to haggle to get you to drop the price. Get all the questions out of the way before showing the price and you will up your percentages.

Chapter 11

MY PILATES SCRIPT

The best victory is when the opponent surrenders of its own accord before there are any actual hostilities...It is best to win without fighting.
Sun tzu

Memorize, Utilize, Maximize Your Success

Mr. *Prospect*, the starting point of Pilates is goal setting. It's about setting a target of what you want to achieve because if you can't see your target, how are you going to hit it? Right?

Have you ever set goals before? What your instructor is going to do is set challenging, believable, achievable goals within a specific time frame, and then put them down on paper so now they become measurable.

Proper food intake also plays a big role. About 40 to 50 percent of your success in the studio is going to be from the things you eat outside the studio. This is especially true if your goal is weight loss. How is your diet right now? How many times per day are you eating? What your instructor is going to do is have you bring in two to three days of your current food intake and supplementation. Do you think that might be something you're able to do?

The third aspect of ensuring your results is the accountability factor. What that means to you is that you will be much more likely to come down to the facility and have quality Pilates sessions when you have an appointment set with a certified professional. If for any reason you don't make it in your instructor will be calling you saying, "We can't accomplish your goals if you're not here!" Can you see how that will benefit you?

And accountability over time works out to be consistency. We know that in anything, if we are not consistent, we are not going to be successful. So your instructor ensures that you adhere to your regular Pilates program in order to accomplish your goals. We recommend that you meet with your instructor two to three days per week for optimal results. How many days will you be able to commit to working with your instructor?

Now, motivation ties into this because your instructor instills in you a greater degree of commitment to accomplishing your goals. Motivation is the difference between accelerated results and just kind of moving along at a slow rate and I'm sure you're like everyone else and you prefer results sooner rather than later, right?

Proper technique also plays a big role. First to avoid injury, and second, if you aren't doing things correctly you will not be able to get the optimal benefits either from the equipment or from your time.

Now, the "personal" in Pilate's session comes in with program design. This involves your instructor designing a customized program for you and monitoring how your body responds so you maximize every rep, set, and minute in the studio to achieve your goals.

Price Prezo

Now, Mr. Prospect, normally a session of Pilates is going to run you $70 per session, but what the company has done to make them more affordable for you as a client is they have grouped them into packages to suit your specific needs. As you can clearly see, the more you show that you are committed to achieving your Pilates goals, the lower the rate per session. The first option is great; it's what I call the starter package. It gives you some time to gain knowledge, learn techniques and how to apply them in the studio so that you can continue to work toward being successful.

Now, Mr. Prospect, I'm going to skip this package for now and move on to what I call our accelerated results package. As you can see, when you enroll in a 32-session package with an instructor the rate drops all the way down to $49 per session. The great thing is that this is the one that our most successful clients are a part of. This package will put you in the optimal position to achieve your Pilates goals through a longer-term commitment and you take advantage of the lowest rate. So you can see that this package is obviously the best value, right? You will really see substantial changes in your body with this package.

Now, I skipped the 16-session package for a very simple reason, Mr. Prospect. This is the most popular package when people enroll in the program on a first-time basis. It's the one that most people in your position go with. It's great because you get a considerably reduced rate and a substantial period of time to work with the instructor and experience the true benefits of the program. During this time you will observe positive results and continued progress.

Now, I will back you up in any decision that you make today toward accomplishing your goals. Out of the different options, which one would you be leaning towards?

Chapter 12

INTRODUCTION TO THE PRE-SCRIPTIVE PRESENTATION

You must be the change that you wish to see in the world.
-Mahatma Gandhi

After you have taken your client or guest through a Pilates orientation they should have some understanding of the benefits of the program. Make sure that you are sitting down and then take a moment to review the orientation card. This way you may refer to and clarify any of the notes that you had taken out on the floor. After finishing a brief outline of the results it is time for you to use your six-step presentation. **This is a very pivotal moment and your success depends upon your diligence in reference to preparation. Do you know the presentation word for word? The difference between success and failure will, in most cases come from ones ability to prepare.** The first part of the presentation should be the benefits building process. The script that I recommend will follow the steps that I have outlined in chapter 10 and will add value to your presentation.

The following is a script that was developed by the same Pilates instructor and regional supervisor at one of the pioneering Pilates studios in California. The revenue and service produced by his Pilates teams still stand up to any modern day challenges. This script has been modified by thousands of Pilates studios world-wide who have used it to produce and generate income from their Pilates departments. Although, I do not endorse or use this script in my studios, it definitely works. As a person in a management position and as a part of a team, I have always felt that it is important to follow a company system. I have worked in many studios that have used this Pilates presentation with great success. Whenever I found myself in a position where a company used or endorsed this presentation I used it as my only form of selling technique. Again, it is important to have a presentation that helps the clients to realize what they are paying their hard earned money for. Therefore, you have to paint a picture in a person's mind of the benefits they will be receiving from your service. If the benefits outweigh the monetary outlay, your clients or guest will be willing the make the trade, money for results.

Closing the Sale

Your prospective client will give you the same objections that you will likely hear when you are trying to sell a package. You will hear everything from "I want to try it out on my own", to "I want to think about it", or "I need to speak to my spouse." It is important to understand that as we are selling anything, especially sales in a Pilates studio, your "be back" sales ratio will be very low. Studies have shown that 60% of customers will say no five times before they will say yes, thus it is important to try to overcome the objections when closing a Pilates presentation. If you are a new Pilates instructor, I would imagine that the most difficult task facing you would be getting and keeping quality clients. You should allocate a percentage of your time every day towards becoming the ultimate in your trade and you must remember to focus on all aspects of being a professional. It is not okay to disregard one area of your arsenal. This is a book on how to sell Pilates. It does focus mainly on selling and retaining a quality stream of income, but it is also a large part of the bigger picture and should ultimately improve your overall success.

Chapter 13

THE SIX STEPS TO A PROFESSIONALLY STRUCTURED PILATES TRAINING PROGRAM

Mr. *soon to be client*, 40-50% of your success in the studio can come from **Food Intake**. "Especially if your goal is weight loss." In order to see optimum results, your instructor will maintain the proper percentage of proteins, carbohydrates and fats. This will ensure satiation. For example: if your goal is weight loss, what your instructor is going to do is work with foods that are convenient for your life style. Based on that information your instructor will customize a caloric deficit. This deficit may consist of a thousand calories a day.

Proper Flexibility and Strength.

Exercise is the stimulus necessary to mobilize fat or excess calories for fuel. Not only is flexibility essential in the prevention of injury but it also ensures that your body maintains its proper elasticity. Your instructor will customize a flexibility and strength exercise program within the proper heart rate zones. This stimulus will create additional lung capacity and circulation. It will also generate muscle toning as a primary focus. Do you see the benefit of that!

As you can see in the first two steps; through proper food intake and proper flexibility and strength exercise, we have eliminated two thousand calories from your body. The laws of thermo-dynamics demand that your body begin to reduce in size and weight. But we have also created the biggest enemy in regards to weight loss. HUNGER. To replace the deficit your body needs nutrients. But most of the time the body fills that nutrient gap with food. The problem with that is, by adding food you also add calories. Therefore change becomes difficult. We will replace the lost nutrients with **Supplementation,** thus creating the prefect environment for change.

Resistance Training.

Your Instructor will design and customize a Pilates workout program specifically for you, muscle equals metabolism. The more quality lean muscle you have, the more your body will continue to burn fat 24 hours a day. I am sure if you are like everyone else you would love to burn fat while you are sleeping.

A vital but overlooked area of your Pilates fitness success will come from **Rest.** During an intense workout session, each and every cell in your body will go through a period of transformation. Without the proper replenishment and rest, your body will be unable to benefit from the exercise. This will ensure full range of motion, rapid recovery, and full muscle development. Do you see the effects of rest?

Professional Assistance.

Along with food intake this may be the most essential part of your fitness success. Your professional instructor will ensure success by manipulating the above five variables so that your body does not level off in regard to the exercise programs. Your instructor will then change and adapt so that you may avoid plateaus and continue to see changes towards accomplishing all of your Pilates goals in and out of the studio.

Chapter 14

PRICE PRESENTATION

The Price Presentation

The price presentation that is used for prescriptive Pilates selling is based on the Pilates instructor being similar to a doctor. The Pilates instructor will lay out details about your goal. Then based on your goal, the Pilates instructor will give you precise information on both the time, and number of Pilates sessions that are required in order to effectively accomplish your goal. Once the instructor has determined the amount of weight loss or muscle gain that the potential client may be interested in achieving, the instructor will then prescribe the number of times per week and the total number of weeks that the client must meet with the instructor. For example, the instructor may say "Mr. Johnson you said that your goal was to lose ten pounds?" Mr. Johnson says, "That's right." "Well, based on our laws of thermo-dynamics, we found that the average person interested in losing weight must meet three times a week with a Pilates instructor." "The average healthy limit for weight loss is about a pound and a half a week." "Based on my professional opinion as your Pilates and weight loss specialist, I recommend that you enroll in a three time a week Pilates program with a certified professional." "Also based on our law of thermo-dynamics you should be able to lose the weight in seven weeks." "Does this make sense to you?" "Yes!" At that point, the instructor will ask; cash, check or credit card. The member usually appears to be somewhat shocked. As the Pilates instructor begins to complete the paper work, the member or client may try to back out of the financial part of the agreement.

Many times, just being assumptive will help create a smooth transition towards completing the sale. This is not my favorite or preferred way to present prices but it is definitely effective. I have spent many years in the Pilates studio business and I have witnessed many things that work and are successful. The goal of my training is not to reinvent nor is it to pick and choose scripts that I think are the best. This Pilates presentation works. It is up to you to decide which presentation best suits your personality and style.

EXAMPLE: x marks the spot for the days and weeks that the client must meet with the instructor.

PILATES GOAL SHEET NO# 1

GOAL_______100% OF YOUR GOAL WEEKS____ DAYS___

PERSONAL TRAINING GAOL SHEET NO# 1 GOAL_______100% OF YOUR GOAL WEEKS____ DAYS___

	Monday	Tuesday	Wednesday	Thursday	Friday	Saturday	Sunday
Week 1	X		X		X		
Week 2	X		X		X		
Week 3	X		X		X		
Week 4	X		X		X		
Week 5	X		X		X		
Week 6	X		X		X		
Week 7	X		X		X		
Week 8							
Week 9							
Week 10							
Week 11							
Week 12							
Week 13							
Week 14							

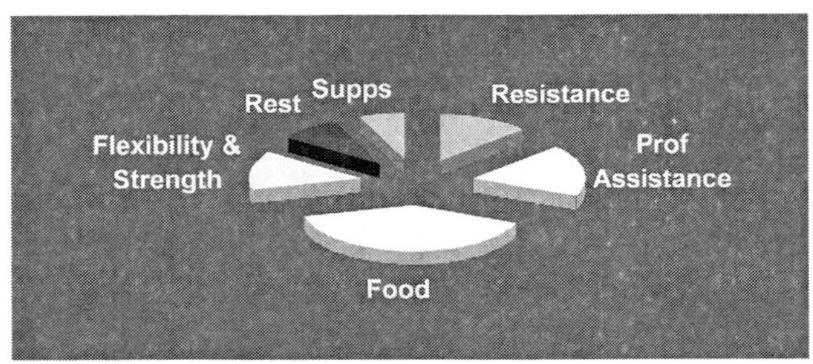

THE HEALTHY ACHIEVABLE LIMIT FOR WEIGHT LOSS IS ABOUT 1 AND A HALF POUNDS A WEEK.

THE HEALTHY ACHIEVABLE LIMIT FOR MUSCLE GAIN IS ABOUT 1 POUND A WEEK.

Chapter 15

THE FISHERMAN

God created man to be successful, yet those who have died as failures could cast shadows on the greatest of pyramids because of their failure to prepare.

The Fisherman

The fisherman realizes it has been a while since he has gone fishing, so he decides that on the morning of the following day he will make a trip to the sea to try his luck during salmon season. He wakes up early, gathers his fishing poles and tackle box, and heads off to "knock them dead." He arrives at the launch ramp and decides to go to the bait shop to buy bait. Unfortunately, the bait shop doesn't open for 20 more minutes, so he gets on the water a little late. When he arrives to his spot, he realizes there are many other fishermen already fishing there. He is frustrated with the amount of competition, but believes there wouldn't be so many people if there weren't any fish. After about an hour trying his luck, he gets his first bite.

He hastily sets the hook to no avail. Frustrated, he changes his bait and takes another cast. This time he hooks a large keeper; he feels like the incredible strength of the large fish may overwhelm him. He fights and he fights and right when he thinks the fish is about to give up, the line snaps. After changing baits several more times the frustrated fisherman hooks into another large fish, and after 20 minutes or so, he brings in his catch. Happy with his accomplishment he packs up his prize and returns home.

The Good Fisherman

The good fisherman realizes it has been a while since he has gone fishing, so he decides that on the morning of the following day he will make a trip to the sea to try his luck during salmon season. He wakes up early in the morning, gathers several fishing poles, tackle boxes, and bait and heads off to "knock them dead." He arrives at the launch ramp at the same time as all the other fishermen and is the third boat on the water. He doesn't need to go to the bait shop, because he bought his bait the night before. When he arrives to his spot, he realizes there are two other boats fishing there. He baits up his fishing poles, and he is into fish after about 20 minutes. Since he has several fishing poles, he puts them at different depths. After about an hour trying his luck, he gets two fish in the boat. He is getting several strikes but seems to be having trouble hooking up. He decides that the problem may be his hooks, and he changes them. This seems to work and he brings in two more fish. Happy with his accomplishment, he packs up his prizes and returns home early.

The Professional Fisherman

The professional fisherman goes fishing almost every day. Fishing for him is more of an addiction than fun. It is a science. The night before the trip he grabs his fishing poles and changes all of the line. He rigs up and sharpens his hooks to a razors edge. He calls the bait shop to find out what time they open, what the fish are biting on, where they are catching them, and at what depth. He then takes a trip that night to the fish market to buy high-quality bait. He wakes up early in the morning, gathers several fishing poles, tackle boxes, and bait. With blood pumping through his veins, he heads off to "knock them dead." He arrives at the launch ramp and is the first boat on the water. Early bird gets the fish. He doesn't need to go to the bait shop because he bought his bait the night before. As he is motoring out to sea, the cool ocean air seems to increase his keen senses. He then notices the birds in the dawn sunlight are diving on some baitfish. He stops under the birds and turns on his depth finder. He lowers his already baited lines to the proper depth, and he is into fish right away. He is a professional at his craft, no down time, lines are always in the water. He has many fish in the boat in a matter of minutes. Happy with his accomplishment, he decides to try different baits, different depths, and different techniques. He catches several different kinds of fish and is happy to try new things. As he returns to the harbor, the other fishermen are packing up to go out and start their day. One of the other fishermen remarks, "Why don't you have any fish in the boat?" The professional fisherman replies, "If everyone keeps their fish, there will be no fish to catch. Catch and release keeps my love for fishing alive." He packs up and returns home early.

The Moral of the Story

The example I have described above can be related to everything in life. Because winning is a habit, losing is also a habit. Losers always lose and winners always seem to win. Losing and wining are equally difficult. Losers have to make up for their losses and have to deal with the repercussions of poor performance. Winners work equally as hard. The difference is that winners do their work and prepare prior to the end goal, and losers do their work afterwards to clean up the mess. One of my mentors once told me, "You can manage yourself by inspiration, or you can manage yourself by desperation." Both being equally difficult, you make the choice. The key points to create winning habits are outlined by the professional fisherman. His first and most important habit is preparation. His second is his love for what he does. His third is his commitment to perfecting his skill. Practice makes perfect. His fourth is his willingness to try new things and broaden his horizons. I wrote this story to help you understand or help you to think for yourself. Question: Are you the fisherman? Think about it carefully. Are you the good fisherman? Are you somewhat prepared? Or are you the professional? The whole package.

Chapter 16

HOW AND WHEN TO *T.O.*

T.O. *(take over)* plays a very important role in the sales learning process. Many sales managers and Pilates supervisors/instructors will use this technique in the mentoring process. Many of the important and vital communication skills that are developed can only be fully understood at the table. Most of these skills are non-verbal and over time you will develop, improve and have the ability to understand all of the non-verbal codes. This will not happen in a day, but in time you may look at someone's face and recognize when they are scared, not comfortable, or in a hurry. Only experience at the table will give you the instincts to tell right away if the potential client is not interested or in a hurry. Likewise you should be able to tell if your client just wants to come in and join and be capable of adjusting your techniques adequately. This is what the TOing process is going to teach you. TOing is going to teach you what to say, when to say it and how to react in every situation. Usually when I am training new staff on how to sell, I will make them get up at least five times from the table during each sales presentation. I do this to advise the instructor of the things to say and do during each step of the selling process. This coaching process enables the Pilates instructor to fully understand all of the variables involved in being the ultimate professional.

Defeat is not defeat unless accepted as reality
- in your own mind!" - Bruce Lee

Examples:

To excuse yourself from the table. "I will be right back." "Let me get the price sheet/business card for you." "If you give me one moment I can find out the answer for you." "Will you please hold on for a moment?" "Let me go and get a pen / calculator."

The client is not going to leave. The reason I ask new salespeople or instructors to do this is because I want to be involved as a manager in the selling process. I want them to inform me as to what is happening at the table. Some Pilates instructors go through the whole sales presentation and don't realize that the client has their spouse waiting for them, or that there has been a price change. Getting up clears the air and gives you the time and space to get advice, it also enables you regroup or think. It is somewhat similar to a timeout used in sports when things are not going well or to gain momentum. You can only learn so much from listening to yourself talk and you should use other strong closers and instructors to add their strong points to your arsenal.

What is lost when you don't TO? You have lost a chance to learn. You have lost a chance to make more money. You have lost a chance to close a sale. All these things are lost when you do not TO. When I was a new salesperson, I asked the other staff and managers to TO for me all of the time. This step was instrumental in my early selling success.

The most important rule of the T.O.

You *cannot talk!* You cannot say anything. Listen, watch, learn, and feel the energy. The only time you should talk is when your potential client tells a lie to the person who is TOing for you, but this is rare. Ensure that your client is sitting down as you will rarely sell a Pilates package if your potential client is standing up. It is imperative to practice and prepare in regard to getting a client to sit down, this will strengthen your closing abilities. Here are some basic rules when TOing.

Rule 1: It is better to TO too early than too late. Do not wait until the guest is leaving, standing up, or totally upset before you TO.

Rule 2: If you are a new Pilates instructor, I recommend that you TO before you give the price. That way, your supervisor will be able to gain the commitment from the guest before showing the price.

Rule 3: TO to your manager, supervisor or top producing instructor. Theses are the people you stand to learn the most from.

Rule 4: Do not be afraid to get up. If your client gives you an objection that you cannot overcome, get up and regroup. ("Hold on just a second, I will be right back.")

Rule 5: Make sure the person TOing for you stays until the completion of the sale. The person may feel like the deal was with the person TOing for you, and may bring up new objections once they leave. (Many sales are lost because of this mistake.)

Rule 6: Make sure that your company is on the same page when it comes to giving information. The last thing you would want to happen is for the person doing a TO to give information conflicting with yours.

Rule 7: The most important rule: You never open your mouth until you know what the shot is! This refers to making sure the person that is doing the TO is aware of what is going on and does not come in and destroy your sale. A briefing prior to the take over will ensure this does not happen

Rule 8: Last but not least **never ever talk**. Once the TO has begun you have given up your right to talk.

Chapter 17

FILLING OUT THE PILATES AGREEMENT

Most Pilates instructors tend to lose their sales right when they begin to fill out the paper work or agreement. Most of the time, the clients will try to stall by asking questions. They are often hoping to find something in your answer they can use to avoid getting started on the program. Some people find it hard to fully agree to the financial terms. You will see many clients that agree with everything you say but then will then try to find excuses at the end of your presentation in an attempt to find a way out of spending any money or starting the program. Remember, the **K-I-S-S** rule **K**eep **I**t **S**imple **S**illy. If you give too much information, the client will find something in your answer that may give them a reason not to get started.

Example: an untrained Pilates professional may say, "We are going to get you up early and start your day off with a protein shake, then we will do one hour of a deep breathing movement session and after that we are going to get you going on flexibility training!" First of all this is not asking a **question** this is making a **statement.** The statement will give the potential client time to "think" of reasons why this won't work. This form of communication lets the clients mind wander! This counterproductive form of communication is the number one mistake made by trainees. In this situation the untrained Pilates instructor thinks that what they are doing is selling, always try to remember *telling is not selling.*

Always fill out the top of Pilates membership agreement with the personal information by yourself. If you give it to the clients, they will stop and hold the pen and start to ask questions. As you fill out the personal information, you want to ask a series of questions that occupy the client's thoughts. If they are answering your questions, their mind is occupied. The thoughts that are going through the mind of the soon to be client are that of **your choosing!** It is now almost impossible for your new client to think of his or her own questions to ask.

For Example:

"It is great that you have decided to join our Pilates program, John. John, could you spell your last name? What is your address, and your telephone number? John, did you want to take care of your training program by cash, check, or credit card? And you brought that with you today?" Simply hold up your hand in the shape of a credit card as you continue to write, and they will almost always reach in and grab their purse or wallet. If they do not reach for their form of payment, ask the same question again, *"And you have brought that with you today?"*

It is important to remember that many of the clients you will be selling to may be in their exercise clothes and were not prepared to make a purchase. Most studios will keep the members credit cards on file or it can be run manually at a later time. At that point, you need to get the client to authorize the Pilates training agreement. You do this by simply explaining the agreement while pointing out each area of the agreement with your pen. I always put circles or stars next to the area that needs to be signed. I explain, "John, this is your Pilates agreement, we have all of your personal information and you will be getting your copy in a moment. Your total investment today is (whatever the total). Your price per session here as you can see is written clearly. I also wrote the total amount just to guarantee that nothing more is charged to your credit card. To guarantee and lock in the discounted rate, just go ahead and give me your authorization there." If they hesitate, simply tap your finger on the dotted line and say, "right here." If they start to read the agreement, simply tap your finger, and say, "John, I will be giving you a copy, and you can read all the rules and details." Again, remember to keep asking questions until all the signatures are finished. "John, did you want to make your first Pilates appointment today or would tomorrow be better for you?" The membership agreement should be controlled by you the instructor and should never leave your hands. It should be filled out quickly while asking questions. After the guest answers each question, follow immediately with another question.

Overcoming the EFT Objections

Many studios will offer the members the use of a charge account and others give the members only one option of paying for the training with cash, check or credit card. Whatever the case may be, most studios will allow the clients to pay for the training in installments. When the clients choose to pay for the package in installments it is important the make sure that payment is "secured." The word secured simply means that we can obtain cash that day if the client doesn't come back! An EFT gives the studio authorization to automatically deduct the amount for the member's Pilates membership from either their checking or credit card account. This helps the member by automatically making their payment and keeping their Pilates active without the concern of making their payment on time. It benefits the studio by having secured access to a check or credit card. This secured billing method is done electronically and uses little time or labor, which will save the studio a substantial amount of money in the long run. It also shows the company's stability to potential investors and/or buyers. When I was new in this business I was so afraid of this kind of payment that the potential clients could sense my fear of EFTs. Remember, a large percentage of communication is nonverbal. If you are afraid of EFTs, your guest will sense it and will not be willing to use this method of payment. Many people have had bad experiences with electronic fund transfers in the past, perhaps you are one of them. Using this system, there is rarely a mistake. I will give you several examples of how to present the easy, no hassle monthly Pilates program.

Example 1:

"Mary, your Pilates package is taken care of monthly, and your bank will send our bank a check automatically each month, sound fair?"

Example 2:

"Mary, I know you have had problems in the past with automatic withdrawal, but wouldn't you rather save your money and earn interest on it rather than paying your Pilates package in full? The new EFT system at our studio is far more advanced than the old systems. It is the safest and the easiest way for you to take care of your training program. I can assure you that if in the unlikely circumstance you were to have any problems you can call me directly, and I will fix it for you immediately. Mary, did you want to pre-pay your package or do our no-hassle plan?"

Example 3:

"Mary, if you do not mind me asking you a question, what would be the difference between the two payment types? You having an EFT monthly for your sessions or coming into the studio to pay are the same thing. The only difference is we do not have the ability to hire a large staff to take all of the client's checks every month. The only difference for you would be if you did not want to pay for your sessions, and you always take care of your bills, right Mary?"

Example 4:

Mary says, "I do not want anyone to have access to my account." I respond, "Mary, the only one who has access to your account is your bank, and you are authorizing your bank to send our bank $150 per month. We have no access to your bank. Any mistake that would be made would be made by your bank and would be your bank's responsibility. Take a look at the agreement, Mary. It shows that you are authorizing only $150 dollars a month on the first of each month and nothing more."

Example 5:

Mary says, "I do not do anything automatically out of my account." I respond, "Mary, I do not do anything automatically out of my account either. But I think you would agree with me that the fees for my checking account are taken out automatically by my bank. Fees for bounced checks or overdraft charges, new check charges, or annual fees are taken out automatically. So I think we can both agree that the future is going to only leave room for this form of payment. Most companies are even deducting taxes automatically from our directly deposited paychecks. So I think you would agree that in most cases, this is our only option."

Remember that an EFT Pilates program is more convenient for the client, the studio, and you. What you as the professional must communicate to the client is that this form of payment exists for their convenience. Like anything else, if they see how the program benefits them and they trust what you say, they will be more likely to agree to it.

Chapter 18

HOW TO OVERCOME OBJECTIONS

The seven most common objections you will hear will be the weaponry used by the clients to stop you from getting them results. These procrastination techniques have been used successfully for years and will prevent you from selling packages. The sooner you learn how to overcome them, the sooner you will be able to start to help people to improve their lives. Getting your clients enrolled in a Pilates package will be almost impossible if you don't learn to overcome the following seven common obstacles.

- Spouse /parent (I want to talk to my husband or wife. Mom or dad.)
- Time (I don't have it.)
- Think about it (I will be back.)
- Try it out (I want to try it on my own.)
- Group/Friends (I have a friend and we want to workout together.)
- Too expensive
- My friend is going to train me.

How long will you wait to learn how to overcome this weaponry? Clients will use the above, as well as other objections against you on a daily basis. The sooner you feel comfortable hearing the excuses and overcoming them, the sooner you can improve as a Pilates instructor. DRILL! DRILL! DRILL!

60% of all sales that are made in the world are only done so, after overcoming five objections!

How to Handle Objections:

1. Hear them out. If you cannot hear the problem, you will not be able to understand their concerns.
2. Feed it back to them in question form, "You want to think about it"?
3. Show empathy. "You want to think about it? I can understand you want to think about it. This is a big decision. "Other serious people just like you, have felt the same way."

Remember Three Key Words:

Feel: "I can understand the way you feel."

Felt: "Other people have felt the same way."

Found: "But what we have found is that once you have started your Pilates training program, it will be the best decision you have ever made."

4. Isolate: "Other than thinking about it, is there anything else preventing you from enrolling in this package today?"
5. Overcome: "What if it was only $10 per session, would you still want to think about it?" "**No?**" "So it is mainly the money."
6. Get it down to money. We cannot control what their husband is going to say, whether or not they want to try it on their own, or whether or not they have the time. But we can change the price. We can work with different package options to fit their individual needs.

Although it is important to use the steps outlined in this chapter, it is also important to know that there are other ways to close a sale. The first closing technique that I teach my instructors is a very simple one. It uses redirection and it is effective when dealing with the right potential client. If you are a new instructor try the 'redirection' technique until you have learned the more complicated ones mentioned in the following chapter entitled 'closing'.

Keeping the Focus on Price

"Out of the different Pilates options, which one are you leaning towards?" **"I want to talk to my husband."** "Did you want to talk to him about the starter package, the accelerated results or the most popular package?" **"I really just want to think about it."** "Did you want to think about the starter package, the accelerated results or the most popular package?" **"I really like the starter package the best but I am not ready to get started until I talk to my husband."** "Did you want to talk to your husband about the price per session or did you want to talk to your husband about the total package price?" **"I want to talk to my husband about the total package price."** "What if I could talk to my boss and get you payment options so that the total package price is more convenient for you, would that make you feel more comfortable?" **"Yes."** If I could talk to my boss and break your package up into payments, would you want to handle your business by cash, check or credit card?" **"Credit card."** "Great and you brought that with you today".

Most objections will center around money. Money is a delicate issue to deal with, so people will avoid talking about it and find other excuses to dwell on. You have seen the excuses above and probably relied on a few yourselves from time to time. Objections are common in this business and you have to learn to overcome them if you are going to be successful.

Chapter 19

CLOSING

It is very important during the closing process to remain calm. Keep your cool and make your guest feel comfortable at all times!

CLOSING

I feel that most instructors would agree that the bottom line in a sale is closing the deal. If everything goes great, you've done everything perfectly but you do not close the sale, the former is irrelevant (if you fail to close the sale then it is irrelevant as to how well you did). Nothing was really accomplished, and no money was made. On the other hand, if you do everything wrong, and you still manage to close every sale, then from a financial and results standpoint, you are successful. That is why people who are closers are held in such high regard in our business today. We can compare this to the quarterback who comes in and throws the touchdown pass in the final seconds to win the game or to the pitcher who comes in to closeout the inning. The people who can get it done are the ones who make big money. No matter how you get there, the end result is to win. This is the reason there is such competition and why so many people in the training business, or who are successful in this trade, are ex-athletes who have thrived and excelled when faced with competition.

There are seven steps used by many of the top producers. These are the areas that when focused on will make the difference between closing every package and missing opportunities. This information is the Holy Grail of the Pilates business. If you follow the advice, you will see a marked improvement in the area of closing. Although I can offer you ideas on what to say, what you say is not half as important as what you do and how you say it. I have TO'ed thousands of sales, and one of the common things I hear from the new Pilates instructors is, and I quote, "You just said the exact same thing I said, and they would not join with me. But they joined with you!" I always reply, "Although we said the same words, you and I communicated something totally different."

Remember to practice these seven steps. Reading them will do nothing for you. We do not sell Pilates to books; these important steps must be practiced in a role-playing situation. Think of it like a football player who studies the playbook. He must know the playbooks forward and backwards to be successful. But simply knowing the playbook is not enough. He needs to put that knowledge to work during practice and games in order to perfect his craft. He must learn to overcome, improvise, and adapt to many different situations as they happen. You are the quarterback of your career. I will provide the playbook, but you must provide the hard work and dedication it takes to perfect it for you to be successful.

The Seven Steps to Closing

1. Close too often and too early rather than too seldom and too late.
2. You must be assumptive. (Always assume the sale!)
3. Use the force, 93 percent of communication is non-verbal.
4. Mirror and match, people feel comfortable with people who are similar to them.

5. Control the conversation with questions. Answer questions with questions.
6. You must overcome five objections. Most of the sales in the world are made only after the fifth closing attempt.
7. Do not be afraid of silence. After asking any question, be quiet, the first one to talk loses the battle

Close too often and too early rather than too seldom and too late!

You want to close too often and too soon rather than too seldom and too late. You do not want to let the opportunity to close a big package pass you by. Closing too soon rather than too late allows you to get a peek at the person's intentions or to gage their interest level. I always say, relatively early in the close, "Which one of these different package options are you leaning towards?" The potential member will tell you which package he or she is considering, and I quickly say "Welcome to Pilates!" It is quick and assumptive, but you may just find the person thanking you and going along with it. If it does not work, the member will usually let you know. It is a gamble worth taking because usually the member will take it as lighthearted and fun and not become too upset. Even if this does happen, you have succeeded in establishing a relaxed situation by making the person laugh. Either way, you are closer to your goal. Here are a couple more examples of questions you can ask to try and close early:

"Were you going to come to your first Pilates session dressed and ready to go? Or were you going to need a locker and a towel?"

I see rookie sales counselors making the following mistake all of the time. "Out of these three package options, which one are you leaning toward?" The member says he likes the starter package. The common mistake that a rookie instructor may make is that they will then ask, "Is the price per session too much or is it the total package price that you are more concerned with?" They have over-anticipated an objection before the member provided one. *Do not do this!* Do not put potentially harmful words in your client's mouth. The potential client just said they were ready to get started, so do not give them the option to now say it is too much. When faced with this situation, all is not lost. You can still overcome this and meet your objective, but you have made it harder on yourself.

The magic "yes" is not going to fall out of the sky. It just does not happen this way. Very rarely does the person say, "I'll take that package." What you want to do is gain their agreement along the way with questions so they are no longer saying no. If they are not saying no, they must mean yes. Assume the sale; you can never close too early.

You Must be Assumptive!

Being assumptive is probably the best close in sales. Just having an assumptive attitude and saying, "Great, welcome to the studio," makes the clients think that it is what everybody does and will simply figure this must be how it works. A lot of the time what we do as Pilates instructors is offer the prospect an opportunity to haggle by not closing the deal right away while we have the opportunity.

I used to work for a person whose favorite close was to show the prospect the different membership options and say, "You know what? I think this one is best for you." Then he would start filling out the agreement. As soon as the person started to talk, he would ask them a question. "Did you want to pay cash or credit card, your first name, last name, address?" and so on. It was so assumptive that he did not even give the person a chance to think it over. He would just start writing. Many times that closing technique worked. But it takes a lot of time to get to that level unless you are just a natural salesperson.

Use the Force!

Use the force to close the sale. This may sound ridiculous to you as a new instructor but, hey, it worked for Yoda. You may think that selling is just pressuring people and talking them into doing something they do not want to do. Actually, sales have little to do with the words that come from your mouth. Think about this: If you were to go into a dark room with another person, is it or is it not a fact that that a person gives off heat? Is it or is it not a fact that that person gives off energy? Is it or is it not a fact that that person makes sounds when breathing or moving? You can even smell them. With no sight and no words, there are many other forces that can affect communication. Behind words, there are certainly many hidden and not so hidden forces. You can insult someone with a smile and it seems like a joke; joke around with him or her with a frown, and it seems like an insult. Only 5 to 10 percent of the message you send consists of the actual words spoken.

Here are some other factors:

1. The tone of your voice.
2. The speed in which you talk.
3. The proximity between you and your guest.
4. How loud you are.
5. Fear in your voice.
6. Your facial expressions. (Many salespeople blush or make faces, and they are not aware they are doing it!)
7. Eye contact.
8. Ability to remain calm.
9. The speed in which you ask or answer questions.
10. The clarity of your voice.
11. Respect level.
12. Using slang.

I think you get the point. I could go on, but I think you are a newfound believer in the force. As I watch my sales area from 30 feet away, unable to hear any verbal communications, I am aware of what is taking place at each and every table. My instructors or Pilates counselors will often ask me, "How did you know what was going on?" I simply say, "I do not have to hear what you are saying; I can see everything you are saying just fine."

Mirroring and Matching!

Remember, people buy from people they like, and people like people who are similar to them. It is important to adjust style and personality to be in touch with your guest. What does this mean? It means having the ability to change the way you act, talk, and the speed in which you react or walk, everything you do to set your rhythm in sync with the person that you are with. This is not something that I can outline for you. It is not something that is easy to teach. But this is an effective tool.

For Example:

If you have a person who is shy, you cannot be aggressive. If you have a person who walks slowly, you cannot walk fast.

This area of your arsenal can go much deeper. You have to be like a chameleon, which is a lizard that can change its color and/or shape to meet its surroundings.

Lead with Questions!

The person asking the questions is the one in control of the conversation. When it comes down to closing a sale, your guest will ask a lot of questions that they do not really care about hearing the answers to. These are stalling tactics. They are looking for something within your answer that would give them a way out. For instance, you are filling out the paperwork, and Mary asks, "Who teaches your step class?" An inexperienced salesperson might answer, "Oh, it is Jonathan; he is one of our best instructors." Mary says, "I do not feel comfortable doing aerobics in front of a man. I think I will just wait." This exact scenario has taken place right before my eyes numerous times. As you can see, if this question was *deaf-eared*, or answered with a question, this would have never become a problem.

Ask for the Sale Five Times!

One of the most effective turnovers in sales is to "go ask them one more time." The reason is, people can give up or change their mind. Sixty percent of all sales that are made in the world are done so after the fifth closing objection. Count how many objections or concerns you field while you are with your next couple of guests. I bet it is more than just two or three. Here is something to think about while handling these numerous objections:

- If you give up on the first objection (some instructors do) you will miss 90 percent of all sales you could have made if you could have handled the five objections.
- If you give up on the second concern (a lot of instructors do), you will miss 80 percent of all sales you could have made if you could have handled the five objections.
- If you give up on the third concern (most instructors do), you will miss 70 percent of all sales that could have been made if only you could have handled the five objections.
- If you give up on the fourth concern (do *you*?), you are missing 60 percent of all the people you could have helped if you just had of asked one more time.

The point is, if you do not have the natural ability to help your guests to feel comfortable or to build rapport, or you fail to use the steps outlined in the "overcoming objections" section, you will never be able to get your potential client feeling comfortable enough to the point where you are able to field several objections without offending them. Remember, sometimes you just have to take the long way around. This may mean getting up from the table and clearing the air, or going back out on the workout floor and re-explaining some of the facilities. Change the scenery for a while. Change the entire subject and try talking for a while about something that has nothing to do with joining a Pilates package. If you are too direct, you will never get to objection number five. Number five is the magic number. It separates the men from the boys, the girls from the women.

After Asking Questions, Shut Up!

The reason we ask questions is to give the potential member the opportunity to think of the answer. If you answer the questions you have asked instead of allowing them to answer for themselves, then you are not letting the guests think on their own and they are certainly not being closed. You must be patient, ask a question and give the guests as much time as they need to answer the question. Once they have answered that question you should be ready with the next question. Do not ever interrupt your guest; the first one to talk loses the battle or in our case (bought it!). Below is an example of a typical situation where you need to ask questions, wait for a response and then be ready for another question.

For Example:

"Mary, why did you come to the studio today?" "I want to tone and gain some lean muscles." *"Mary, if you do not mind me asking, you look great to me, why did you want to gain some lean muscles?"* "I just saw a picture of myself, and I cannot believe how flabby I looked." *"How did you feel when you saw that picture, Mary?"* "I couldn't believe it! I decided right then and there that tomorrow I was going to gain some lean muscles." *"Mary, if I could show you the perfect program to help you gain lean muscles and feel great about yourself in the shortest time possible, would you be interested in getting started today?"* "Absolutely!" *"Mary, did you want to go ahead with the package that includes our Pilates and nutrition or would you just prefer to go with our basic Pilates training program today?"* "I will take the instructor and the nutrition." *"Welcome to the studio!"*

Closing Types:

The Verbal Closing: "If I could, would you"

Of all the closes I can think of, this one is still one of the best. It is, "If I could, would you..." This means that if I could get that for you today would you want to get started. You always want to be two steps ahead of the other salespeople.

For Example:

"You know, we used to have this program. I do not know if I can still get it for you, but I can talk to my manager. I do not know if he will go for it, but if I could *talk to him and see if I could get that for you,* would you *be interested in getting started today?"*

In many cases you will show the potential client your training options and they will say they want to think about it. What you need to do is mention the package that was just available, but has since expired. Then you can offer the "if I could, would you" close.

The "If I could, would you!"

"Out of the different Pilates packages which one are you leaning towards" **"I need to think about it!"** "I can understand you want to think about it but if you were to pick one, which one would it be?" **"Probably the middle one."** "You know we had a special package option for that particular program, but it has expired! Earlier today my boss authorized one of these for one of our VIP members, if I could go talk to my boss and get this kind of option would you be interested. **"What was the special price?"** "It was 16 sessions at $40 per session. I could ask my boss. I'm not making any promises but the worst thing he can do is say no?" **"Go ask?"** "If my boss says yes how will you pay, cash or credit card?" **"Cash!"** "And you brought that with you today?"

Two sales, One client

This close I am going to tell you in story form. I see so many Pilates instructors make the mistake of not taking the opportunity of turning one sale into two or three sales. This happens because of a very simple reason: They never ask for it. I travel back and forth from the United States to Taiwan on a regular basis. Since I live in Nevada, I usually have a lay over in San Francisco. There is a young boy there who is great at shining shoes. He is a master at his trade.

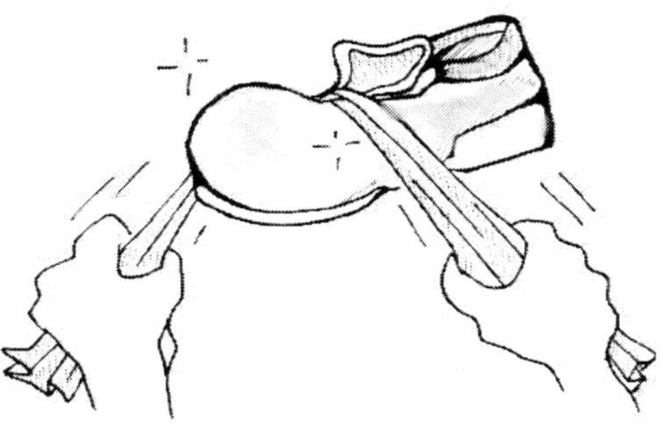

He puts a lot of flare into the art of shoe shining. As I arrive at the San Francisco Airport, I see that he is working. I go over to him and ask him how much it is for a shoeshine.

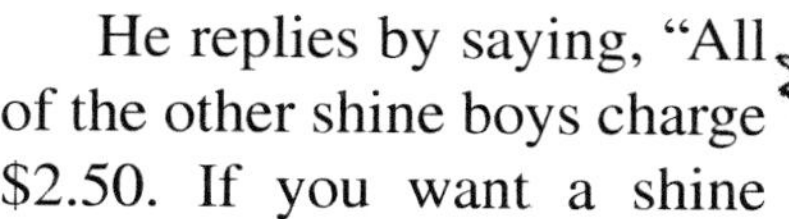

He replies by saying, "All of the other shine boys charge $2.50. If you want a shine from me, it is going to cost you $3. It is a little more but I guarantee you, you will know where that extra 50 cents went." Then he turns his eyes down towards my shoes, and he says, "Those look like a pair of expensive shoes." I say, "Yes, they are. They cost a lot of money." Then he replies to me, "Why don't you buy a cheaper pair of shoes, like ones from discount shoe stores?" I respond by saying, "Quality is important to me. I believe you get what you pay for." He looks me in the eyes, smiles, and responds by saying, "Then I guess you want to have your shoes shined by me." I smile and take a seat in the chair. He opens up his box and starts to shine my shoes.

Each time the towel hits my shoes, it makes a popping sound. He has perfected this trick over the thousands of shoes he must have polished. He spins the towel and hums and appears as if he is singing a song with the friction and popping coming from the towel. He then looks down at the bottom of my shoes and says to me, "These are Italian leather shoes, and I must admit they are some of the nicest I have ever seen."

As he comes to the finish, I can see he has done an excellent job shining my shoes. He looks at me and he says, "You know I have something in my box that they made just for expensive Italian shoes just like these. It may cost you 50 cents more, but your shoeshine will last twice as long. Do you want to go with the Italian lotion or did you just want me to finish up with the cheap stuff?" By now, I am sure you can guess my answer. Just by the way that he phrased his questions and the confidence he did it with, I was sold. A professional salesman being closed by a boy. He then does something that most experienced salespeople often forget to do. He asks me how long my lay over will be. I respond by saying that I will be in the airport for another couple of hours before taking off for my home. He then asks me if I have to dress up for work every day. I respond by saying, "Yes, unfortunately, I have to wear a suit and tie to work." The boy then responds by saying, "Do you wear the same pair of shoes every day?" I say, "No, I have different colored shoes for the different suits that I wear." As I see the wheels in his head turning, he looks at me and says, "If you have other shoes with you, I will be willing to shine them as well. Not only that, but I will be willing to put the expensive Italian lotion on them for free, sound fair?"

Without giving me the time to respond, he follows up by saying, "Leave your shoes here for me, go grab something to eat, and they will be ready in 20 minutes." Whether I say yes or no is not the point, the point is that he asked. He turns one sale into three, and he adds 50 cents with the lotion. I am sure that not every person says yes, but if 25 percent of the people do, he increases his sales by a large percentage. Do not forget to *up-sell.* Who says you can't learn a lot from a child?

Are you aware of the fact that McDonald's Corp. increased their sales 25 percent by simply asking one question: "Would you like fries or a coke with that?" They took it even one step further by asking people if they would like to "Super Size" their fries and cokes. They take the sale one step further by changing their menus from having all the different foods listed on the menu to having meal deals on the menu. Instead of having to pick just the hamburger or just the french-fries, they all come together in a meal for one low price.

The Lost Sale Close

The *lost sale* close is one you can use when your potential client is in the parking lot. It is a last ditch effort when everything else has failed. It starts with first letting the member know that you are aware they are not going to join on a package today but you were just letting them know that this is how you earn a living. Tell them that their feedback is important to you improving your craft and ask them some questions.

For Example:

"What did I do wrong? I must have done something wrong? I can't help anyone get started. I just want to help people and no one wants to help themselves. Is it me? Is something wrong with me? Did I do something to offend you? Maybe I am just not cut out to help people. Maybe those other used car salesmen inside were right. Maybe I should quit being so nice and just start taking people's money. Forget about their goals and dreams."

I know, I know, it is a pretty low move. It is also pretty shameless, but believe it or not, this method does work from time to time. Hopefully you do not find yourself in any situations where you have to resort to a tactic like this. If you do find yourself in that situation, it is good to have a script ready.

Keeping the Focus on Price

"Out of the different Pilates options, which one are you leaning toward?" **"I want to think about it."** "Did you want to think about the starter package, the accelerated results or the most popular package?" **"I really just want to think about it."** "Did you want to think about the starter package, the accelerated results or the just the most popular package?" **"I really like the starter package the best but I am not ready to get started until I talk to my husband."** "Did you want to talk to your husband about the price per session or did you want to talk to your husband about the total package price?" **"I want to talk to my husband about the total package price."** "What if I could talk to my boss and get you payment options so that the total package price is more convenient for you, would that make you feel more comfortable?" "**Yes.**" If I could talk to my boss and break your package up into payments, would you want to handle your business by cash or credit card?" **"Credit card".** "You brought that with you today?"

The Alternate Choice

The *alternate choice* is what we do when we show the member all of the different package options and then say, "Would you want to go with option one or would you prefer option two? Out of the different options which one are you leaning toward? Did you want to start today or would tomorrow be better for you? Do you want your membership with a male instructor or a female instructor?" The alternate choice is a simple and effective close. In sales, you will learn that if you give somebody two choices they are going to take one of them. "Did you want to go with cash, check or credit card?" It has been around forever and works in all types of businesses. Learn it and get used to it because you will see that you will probably use this close as much as, if not more than any other.

The Ben Franklin Close

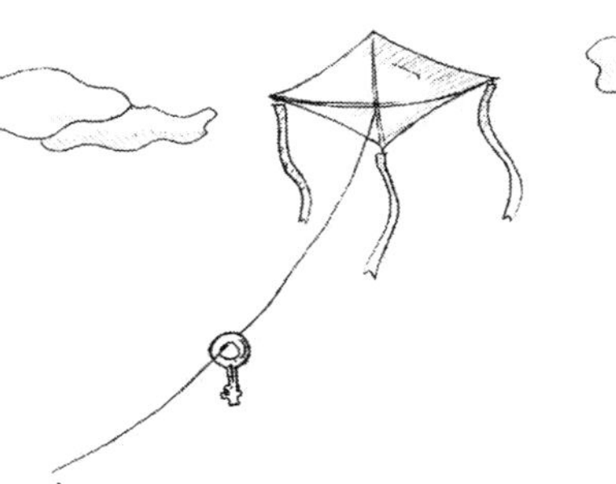

This close is especially good for closing a Pilates package. This close involves developing a plus *vs.* minus system. This close does not necessarily have to be a Pilates studio close as it can be used for anything that you are trying to sell. What really matters is that you have the positives and the negatives of why the potential client should make a decision. It is very effective but do not be afraid if it takes a while as you may have to go through a little bit of a process in order to make this happen.

Ben Franklin, one of our countries founders had to make a number of complicated decisions, fortunately for us, he was a smart man. Whenever Ben Franklin had to make a difficult decision he would list the positives and the negatives of why he should make that decision. He would make a list of all the reasons why he should do it and all the reasons why he should not do it. Based on the positives against the negatives, he would weigh it out and decide if he should make the decision or wait for a while before deciding. If the positives outweighed the negatives, he would make that decision and *vice versa*. If there were a clear distinction between the two then he would choose the one with the most points in its favor, be it positive or negative.

It is really quite simple, all you need to do is write the answers to questions given by the customer onto a piece of paper. Title one side of the paper, *Positives* and the other side of the paper, *Negatives*. Ask the customer, "What positives do you think will come from you becoming healthier and gaining some lean muscles?" The answers will vary and include such positives as health, looking good, lower blood pressure, feeling better, strengthen the heart, increased energy and stamina, and so on. If they do not come up with enough give them a couple of more positives so you can fill up that column. Do not give them too many because you want them to see their answers on the paper. After writing down about ten to twelve positives, move over to the negatives. Ask the customer, "What are some of the negatives you can see as a result of getting in shape and improving your health?" The funny thing about the question is that there is no acceptable answer to it.

Whatever you do, do not help them fill out this side of the paper, they will have a hard enough time finding any answers so do not help them. You will receive answers such as, "I don't have the time" or "I don't have the money," two of the easiest objections to overcome. That is about it. You have not only showed them that the positives outweigh the negatives, you have also uncovered a couple of objections. Your next step is to read back all of the positives and then the negatives. Your closing question will be something like, "Mary, wouldn't you agree that sacrificing an average of one hour of your time and few bucks is a small price to pay to be able to live longer, look better, have more energy, lower you blood pressure, sleep better, and more?" (Simply read back their positives.)

You have now made it obvious that their objections have been squashed underneath the pressure of all of the positives they are going to receive. You have built value within the product and shown that they need to listen to you in order to achieve their goals, that the only way to get all of the positives is to get started on the program. Once they have seen that, they find it hard to say no because it is simply not a logical answer. It takes a little longer than some of the other closes but it is well worth it.

Motivational Speaker

"Mary, last week I went to a seminar featuring a motivational speaker. He explained that the reason people are unhappy with their life is that they spend a lot of time and energy worrying about the little things and they fail to take care of the big things. He said and I think that you will agree, that there are four major areas in your life and if you take care of these four areas, then the rest of your life will be more enjoyable. They include your relationships (friends, family, and loved ones), financial stability, spirituality, and your health. He explained that these four things affected each other. Having no friends or family could affect your health. Having poor health could affect your job. Having no spirituality could affect your ability to care or have a meaningful life. Now, Mary, I do not know if the motivational speaker was right or wrong, but I think you would agree with me that without your health, nothing else really matters."

The Negative Take-Away Close

I found that this close works extremely well with a person that shows little interest or emotion. You have to find something in this individual that will stimulate action. I found that sometimes the only way to do this is by taking something away. You may find that your clients say that they are not really interested in getting started on a package. They are not really interested in exercise, and they never thought about practicing Pilates before. It is going to be hard for you to gain commitment if you cannot get your client's attention. You may simply state that it is okay and that even if they wanted to get started on a package today it would be impossible for you to sign them up. Tell them that unfortunately, at this time, the studio is full of members that care about being healthy. You may recommend putting them on a waiting list and giving them a call back when there is an opening for you to take more clients. This may spark something in them that makes them want something they cannot have. The guest may be using this technique to try to get you to beg them to get started. When you do not show interest, they will be surprised. This will cause them to loosen up on their objections and force him or her to show an interest in order to get what you will not give him or her. In many cases the prospective client will try to buy their way through the waiting list.

Magic Potion

I use this close quite often for people who believe that there are shortcuts to becoming healthy. Trendy diets, weight loss retreats, starving, steroids, all of these are worthless without exercise and a good diet and yet people still waste their time trying them. You have to use a little bit of imagination and have a fairly good rapport with your client.

Ask your client to think of a time when they were in the best shape of their life. Make them think about the time when they felt great, looked great, and people would comment on their accomplishments. Then pick up a cup or a bottle of white out and look at the client and say, "What if I had a magic potion that you could drink and when you awoke the following morning you would have the perfect body? If I had a potion like that, how much do you think I would be able to sell it for?" You can ask your client, "If I had a potion like that, how much will you be willing to pay for it?"

Your client may respond by saying, "That would be priceless. You can sell it for any amount." I respond by saying, "So you would agree that your body is also priceless? You and I both know there is no quick fix, there is no magic potion. Believe me, if there was,

Oprah Winfrey the richest woman in the country would not be overweight. The only way for you to have the perfect body is for you to adjust your lifestyle to include your priceless body."

The Magic Potion close works to get the client to understand that there is no easy way to losing weight and maintaining their health. This close must only be done with those clients with whom you have built a strong rapport. If you try it with someone who you do not have a good rapport with, they will not follow along and will miss the point of the presentation.

The Only Car You Will Ever Have

When I first started in sales, this close was one used by a good friend of mine. Personally, I have never used it, but it seemed to work very well for him. He would simply ask the client a series of questions to make the client realize how important health and fitness was. He would compare the person's body to an automobile. He would state, "John, I want you to imagine, you are living in a foreign country. And in this country, there is a rule; the rule is that you are only going to have one automobile to last for your entire lifetime. The rule is put in place to teach people to take care of things and be responsible. On your 21st birthday, you are given your one automobile to have for your lifetime. Would you change the oil in your automobile? Would you keep your automobile clean? Would you put the best gasoline in it? Would you put the protection on the rubber and leather? I am sure you would agree with me, if you were only going to have one automobile for the rest of your life, one of your highest priorities would be to take care of it. Wouldn't you agree? John, the reason I ask you these questions is in relation to your body. You only get one body; you will never ever have a chance to get another one. I think you would agree that having one body is more important than having one car."

This is a very successful close. The entire time you are working to gain the agreement of your client. Once they have realized the point or the correlation between the story and their body, it becomes almost irrational for them to say no. This must only be done if you have built a strong rapport with the client. If you do not, much like the Magic Potion close, they will not gain the significance of it.

Benefits Not Bashing

One of the most important techniques used in sales today is focusing on the benefits. How is our product going to benefit the customer? Why it is important for the customer to have the product? Why does the customer need it? How does our product differ from other products? All of these questions need to be addressed before you are going to make a successful sale. The goal is to cut down on everything but the pure benefits. It is important to use our three-step method, statement of fact, two to three questions and a tie-down.

For Example:

"*John, now I have explained the benefits of our Pilates program, I think you would agree that no other instructor can offer you a program to compare with mine.*" It is important not to knock other instructors; it can ruin your credibility. When a client talks about the benefits of another instructor, I simply agree and say "*John, Tommy is a very nice instructor, and I think you would agree that he has a very good price. But what I would like to do is take a moment of your time to tell you the benefits of my program, as well as the best price, and let you make the decision for yourself, sound fair?*"

By doing this, you are keeping the client interested in your abilities. You are allowing them to make their own decision but asking them in a way that only the answer "yes" will benefit them. Remember, you are there to make them happy. If you are looking out for their interests and trying to find benefits for them, they will appreciate it and you will have a stronger rapport.

The "Thinking About It" Close

This objection is at the tip of every client's tongue if they are going to give one. If a person gives you this objection, they are in a situation where they are searching for a way out of committing, most likely to try to avoid spending money. It is what we call a "secondary objection" because it is often used to hide another. When the situation arises, stay calm and remember this close.

For Example:

"I can understand you want to think about it. Other people have felt the same way that you feel. What we have found is that most people have already thought of everything there is to think about. Then what ends up happening is you go home, you walk towards the door, you pick up your mail, and you start thinking about the bills you have to pay. You go in and listen to your answering machine, turn on the TV, get busy with the dinner and kids. One thing leads to another, and all of a sudden, it is six months down the road, and you really have not gotten back around to doing what you originally had the best intentions of doing today. Every morning we wake up and have the best intentions of doing all of the things that are going to make our life better. It just seems by noon, or half way through the day, our mind has tricked our bodies into making the wrong decision, into procrastinating, waiting, or putting it off until tomorrow. I think you would agree, that the time is right, and now is the time. What better place to think about it? You have all the information that you need on the table, you have an environment that is free from distraction, and you have me here to answer all of your questions."

It is quite a bit to remember but it is the only close you are going to need in this situation. You will find that people will make objections, such as this one, just because they are afraid to commit to anything. When they are in a situation where they cannot find anything they truly object to, they will fall back on their old-reliable "I want to think about it."

The "What about this? What about that? What if I could?" Close

I have found that the most effective close is just offering the guest different options until you find one that works for them. Most of the time, your guest is not going to tell you the real reason as to why they are not getting started. They will come up with objections instead of telling you the real reason they are not joining the studio is that you, the professional, have not yet found a training option to fit their needs. I read a great book about sales not long ago that really opened my eyes. Two salesmen wrote this book, and it only contained facts and figures on what motivated people to make a purchase.

They put hidden cameras in sales offices all over the world and studied what the key points involved in the person's final decisions were. More interesting to me was when they focused on what the different salespeople did in different situations when confronted with different objections. The two biggest factors were No.1, the salesperson never asked for the sale, and No. 2, they could not find an option that met the customer's needs. Many salespeople today cannot close a sale because they do not understand the fact that the one or two options that they are offering are not working for the customer.

For Example:

"Mary, this package option includes a one time total investment of 500 dollars, leaving your balance investment at only $250." "I need to think about it." *"Mary, let me ask you a question, is taking care of your package in full an option for you?"* "I still want to try it first." *"Mary, what if I could get you a smaller package that would give you an opportunity to try the training program, as well as a little more time to see the benefits exercise will have on you?"* "That sounds a little better." *"I have a 3session option for $120 and I have 5 session option for $200. Both of them would give you some time to see changes in your body. At the end of that your package will expire. If you decide you like the program, and you are seeing*

results we could talk about a longer term commitment. I think this may answer all of your concerns. Out of option 1 and option 2, which one would you be leaning towards?" "Option 2." *"Mary, welcome to the one on one Pilates training program. Your address? Phone number? Would you be handling your Pilates packages by cash, check or credit card?"* "Credit card." *"And you brought that with you today?"*

The example I have given above shows that Mary really did want to get started. I simply had to find a package option that elevated her concerns and met her needs. This is very common in our business. Many times it is not that the guest does not want to enroll, it is that the guest has not seen anything that they really feel comfortable with. The reason most successful instructors and studios have multiple package options is so they can tailor them to suit many different people and their individual needs. It is your job to find the best one for each situation.

The "Just Do It" Close

I hate to say it, but sometimes just saying the words, "*Oh, come on, just do it!*" will be motivation enough for some people to enroll. I do not know why this works, but it does. I do not know how many times this close has been used in high schools to get an under-aged kid to drink his first beer. The words, "*Oh, come on, just do it!*" work.

You must have a good rapport with your guest to use this one. It is playful, yet effective. Many people simply need to have somebody there to give them that extra shove to get them going.

My Grandma Close

This close works very well with senior citizens and long-time procrastinators. You will often find yourself unable to get older people to even answer any of the questions. When this happens, I change gears and go from sales mode to story mode. I simply sit down at the table and say, "*John, I know that you are not interested in making a decision today. You know there is a little story I would like to tell you, it would only take a minute of your time if you do not mind. I wanted to tell you the reason I had for getting into this business. When I was in my early 20s, I was still very active in sports and was very serious about making it to the studio on the daily basis. At the time, I was concerned with looking great and feeling great and I truly could not understand why anyone would choose to not exercise Pilates. At that time, I had a grandmother who was in her early 60's, and was in pretty poor physical condition. She worked long hours; her diet included a steady supply of cheese, chips, coffee, cigarettes and aspirin. Several times a week, I would stop by her house on my way to the gym and raid her refrigerator. On my way out, I would ask her, 'Grandma, why don't you go to the gym with me today? There are lots of other people there just like you, and they feel great about their Pilates training programs.' She would always respond by saying, 'I am busy', or 'Not today, I will go with you tomorrow.' She would give me every excuse in the book. As the years went by, she seemed to have less energy, more health problems, and an overall, lackluster outlook on life. So finally one day, I walked in her house, I put her in a headlock, I literally dragged her, kicking and scratching into the studio with me. After taking a 15-minute stretching and some light resistance training, my grandmother had seemed to be reborn. She spoke to some of the other seniors in the studio, and they gave her a schedule for the senior classes. After leaving the studio, she felt energy and vigor that she had not felt in years. My grandmother has continued on a Pilates program three days a week for the past seven years. If you were to ask her about her physical condition, she would tell you she feels better at 70 than she felt at 40. John, if I let you leave the studio today with out a Pilates training package, I would be going against everything that my grandmother believes was the best decision she ever made. She still reminds me of the day that I dragged her to the car and dragged her into the studio, and it reminds me of the joy of helping someone, like yourself, do what you know you should do right now!*"

Overcoming Objections

I am going to give you two or more ways to overcome each of the objections.

"Spouse (I want to talk husband or wife, Mom or dad.")

Option 1

"I want to talk to my wife." "You want to talk to your wife?" "Yes we have an agreement whenever we do anything in regard to money we talk it over!" "I can understand that, I am married too and this is a big decision. I know you wouldn't even be considering talking to your wife if you weren't **very** serious. Let me ask you one question, other than talking to your wife; is there any thing else holding you back from getting started to day?" "No." "Let me ask you this Larry, if the Pilates package was three dollars a session would you be able to make a decision today with out your wife." "Yes." "So you can spend money without talking to your wife, just not a lot of money, is it the price per session or the total package price that is too much." "It is the total package price!" "So if I could talk to my boss and get your package price reserved with a small deposit and you could go home and talk to your wife would that work for you?" "Yes." "How much could you put down today to hold this price?" "Half." "Okay Larry let me go talk to my boss." "Larry how do you normally handle your business, cash check or credit card?" "Credit card." "You brought that with you today?"

Option 2

"You go call your husband and see if he will let you purchase the package, and I will call my wife and see if it is okay for me to sell the package to you."

Option 3

"Your wife is going to say no?" "No, my wife isn't going to say no." "Well, she doesn't care; she probably won't want you to spend money." "Is she going say yes?" "If you are so sure your wife will say yes, then you really don't need to ask her?"

Option 4

"Your body has nothing to do with any other person other than you. Your husband/wife cannot workout for you or tells you not to work out. Your body is yours, and it is 100 percent your decision. Buying a car or a house is different, because it is communal property. Your body belongs to you and it is your decision if you want to be healthier or feel good about the way you look. No other person can make that decision, wouldn't you agree?"

"My friend is going to train me."

Option 1

"I understand that you have a lot of confidence in your friend. I think you would agree with me when I say that going through a couple of Pilates sessions can give you a better understanding of whether or not your friend has a Pilates training program that can get you the results that you are looking for."

Option 2

"I appreciate the fact that you feel that your friend is a great Pilates enthusiast. I should also remind you that our company policy requires all the instructors to have a certification and insurance coverage to operate in this studio."

"I don't have time"

Option 1

I usually quickly respond by saying, "you don't have time not to!"

Option 2

"John, you have already made an incredible investment in regards to the time and amount of money that you have put aside for Pilates, if time is a concern, I can show you that I specialize in Pilates programs that give you more results in less time. Now you will have more time."

"I want to try it on my own"

Option 1

"John, I understand that you want to try it on your own; I also understand that you have had success in the past. Pilates is a relatively new concept and fitness in regards to what works and what does not. Some of the new information that I have to offer can help you get results quicker and easier and I'm sure if you are like everyone else, you would like to make your workouts quicker, easier, and more effective."

Option 2

"John, when I was in my early 20's, I decided to take up golf. I went out and bought an expensive set of golf clubs, and despite the pro shop advice, I refused having a pro give me some pointers. In time, I developed a very interesting new system for making the ball curve when I hit it. When I finally decided to go in and see a professional to make an adjustment, it was extremely difficult for me to change my bad habits. If I had learned to play golf the right way in the beginning, I would have been well adjusted by this time. I implore you not to make the same mistake or pick-up the same bad habits that I did."

"I want to think about it"

Option 1

"I can give you three days to shop around. If for any reason you find any other studio that offers better reliability or you like better, come back to get a full refund, and I can still give you a discount by starting today. There is nothing to lose!"

Option 2

"Mr. Prospect, you want to think about it? I can understand you want to think about it. I understand how you feel. Other people have felt the same way, but what we have found is that by joining on a package today, it will be the best decision you will ever make in your life. Other than thinking about it, is there anything else to stop you from joining a Pilates package today?" "No." "May I ask you a question? How many days are you going to need to think about?" "Two days." "What if I could give you two days to think about it, and still give you a discount on your package by starting up today? I could give you a discount today and you would have three days to decide to keep your Pilates training package or get a refund. Sound fair?"

Option 3

If it is over the telephone: "I want you to go to all the other studios in town, make sure you take notes about the different price options and packages that are provided by the other studios. Then, I want you to come to our office with the information. I will prove to you that our business can beat any other business when it comes to the services that we provide. Not only that, but I will also beat any other price. I think you would agree this is the right way to make the most educated decision. Would morning or evening be best for you?"

"Group/friends" "I have a friend and we want to take sessions together."

Option 1

"It is true working out with a friend can offer some great benefits, in most cases I found that in modern day society, with jobs and families, and all the things going on, sometimes being consistent with a partner can be impossible. Why don't we get you started with a 3-session package, and if your friend is interested, they can join us during our sessions."

Option 2

"Not only do I specialize in Pilates and nutrition, but I also specialize in group training sessions. If you would be interested, I might be able to talk to my boss and include a program that would teach you and your friend how to train together and how to accomplish your goals in the shortest amount of time possible. If I can talk to my boss and teach you and your friend how to benefit from group training, how would you handle your business: cash, credit card, or check?"

"It's too expensive."

Option 1

You can break it down to the ridiculous price, most of the time it will be, "*Your Pilates session is $20 per month, how much too much is it?*" "It is $5 too much." "*So $5 is stopping you from joining the studio today?*" "Yes." "*Five dollars divided by 30 days equals 16 cents per day, so 16 cents per day is stopping you from becoming healthier? Don't you think your health and happiness is worth 16 cents per day?*"

Option 2

"It's too expensive" is the best objection we can get. Out of all of the other objections, it is truly the one we have the most control over. We cannot control what their husbands are going to say, cannot control how convenient the studio is for them. But we certainly have control over different Pilates package options and prices available to them. You must learn how to handle this objection with many different tactics. If you do not, you will lose a large number of potential sales. You are going to hear it, so you better start practicing for it.

Option 3

"Out of the different Pilates options, which one are you leaning toward?" "it's too expensive." "Was it the starter package, the accelerated results or the most popular package that was a little more than you were looking to spend?" **"I really just think that it is a little out of my price range."** "Which one of the packages is a little bit too much, the starter package, the accelerated results or the just the most popular package?" **"I really like the starter package the best but I am not ready to get started until I talk to my husband."**

"Did you want to talk to your husband about the price per session or did you want to talk to your husband about the total package price?" **"I want to talk to my husband about the total package price."** "What if I could talk to my boss and get you payment options so that the total package price is more convenient for you, would that make you feel more comfortable?" **"Yes."** If I could talk to my boss and break your package up into payments, would you want to handle your business by cash or credit card?" **"Credit card".** "You brought that with you today?"

You will get objections, everybody does. The best are the ones who have enough in their arsenal to overcome a variety of different objections and attitudes with a variety of different tactics and personalities. If you want to be the best, you must learn to overcome objections. The few that I have detailed for you will be the most common. Learn them, overcome them, and be the best.

Chapter 20

MY FIRST EXPERIENCE AS AN INSTRUCTOR AND THE RON FLETCHER STORY

"Pilates is a kind of Western-methodized version of yoga concepts, using specialized equipment for stretching, strengthening and isometric exercises in which muscles develop tension without allowing them to cause actual movement. Pilates also combines a psychological component with the exercises and is very effective for some people.

As a new Pilates instructor, you will spend many hours studying detailed Pilates physiology. You may spend a substantial amount of time learning the intricate functions of the human body. As your Pilates education progresses you will learn how to schedule and juggle your different Pilates routines. After completing these difficult tasks, you will have an opportunity to go out into the real world. For most instructors this is the time when you may begin to observe your educational shortcomings and the answers during this difficult time may be rather elusive.

When I was a young student studying to get my degree, I had made a decision that after I completed my education that I would go into a Pilates or fitness type of career field. After studying for years and learning everything I possibly could about my field, I found myself getting ready to enter the working world. After doing some research, I found that the best fit for me would be working for a large Pilates studio organization, one that had high volume, a good earning potential, the possibility of getting promoted and different locations in different cities. The most important aspect of working for a larger and more seasoned organization would come in the form of a comprehensive training program. When I started the process of interviewing and applying for different companies, the main focus of the employer had little to do with my educational background; in fact it seemed almost irrelevant. Some of the questions that were coming out of the mouths of the potential employers were rather shocking.

The first place I went to apply was a chiropractor and rehab center that had sort of a fitness style Pilates studio in the back. It was a well known and established and had a good reputation. I had a chance to meet with one of the partners and he told me that all the instructors had great earning potential. The only problem came from the fact that the job paid zero base salary and the instructors were expected to work for free until they had built a certain number of clients. Not only was this odd to me, but the clinic also required that we pay for our own advertisements. The partner also stated that we were not allowed to use their customers as new clients!

After determining this was not the best option for me, and feeling this was just an odd system, I decided to go to one of the large well-known Pilates studio chains. After going through an initial interview process with the head Pilates instructor, I then had an opportunity to meet with the regional fitness director. The first words out of the director's mouth was, **"Sell Me Pilates."** I explained that I had not gone through an official sales training courses and I was not particularly interested in becoming a sales person. The regional training director told me that in a Pilates studio, every employee in every department must have the ability to sell.

After going to several interviews, I found that all of the different organizations that I was trying to approach had one thing in common, "Making Money." After dedicating several weeks, and many frustrating hours, toward the grueling task of getting someone to believe that I could help Pilates studio clients get results, I determined that maybe being a Pilates instructor was not something that was going to be in my future.

Upset and a little frustrated and maybe feeling like it was time to give up, I decided to go back and double check the agenda and text material that had been such an intricate part of my learning process. Maybe I was sick for the week of the certification program that covered selling. Maybe I was not paying attention when the teacher talked about the needs and wants of future employers. After spending significant time on research, I realized the structure for selling and retaining or even acquiring new clients simply wasn't present in any of the training material that I was provided. Why would an organization dedicated to teaching such an honorable trade pay absolutely no attention whatsoever on how to make money or how to get a job.

I decided that drastic times called for drastic measures. I had a close friend who had worked in the executive level of a large Pilates studio organization. He had since moved on to other things, but had maintained a great reputation for being a top producer in the Pilates studio business and was still highly respected. I asked if we could meet and if he would assist me by answering some of the questions that I thought would help me in my quest to find out how these organizations functioned.

"Why don't other professionals such as physical therapist or chiropractors have to sell?" "Who told you those guys don't have to sell? The main difference between the chiropractors that make 100,000 and the one that make 30,000 is their ability to sell. Most of those guys don't even make it through their first year because they give up when faced with what you are going through right now."

"Why do the instructors have to sell?" "It may not be that they want you to be a great salesman, they just want to know that you are open to the fact that money is an important part of any business. A Pilates studio or rehabilitation center is a business first and foremost. Nobody can offer a business service if they can't pay their electricity bill. Would you work for free?" I responded by saying, "of course not!" This answer really made sense to me"

"Why is selling such a high priority?" "Selling is such a high priority for the company because of the following factors. This is a Pilates studio and the goal of the Pilates studio is the same as those of the guest or the clients, it is to get results. It is to get bigger, better, faster, and stronger. This is what kind of employees they are looking for; they want to know how you can help each and every clients get results. Can you get a client results in 1 or 2 sessions? Can you get a client results if you can't get them to show up to their sessions. Can you get a client results if you can't get them to change their poor life style? Can you get a client results if you can't get them to start Pilates? You have to be able to sell every aspect of Pilates or procrastination will win."

"Why do these companies pay so little as a base salary and such a high commission?" "In a Pilates studio most people that work with instructors are doing so because they are not self motivated or because they want someone who will push them. Most of these individuals will not make the initial move when it comes to asking for the service. In most cases, even if they do ask they will procrastinate about getting started without a little push. The studio benefits the most from clients that get results and this may not happen if the client is not encouraged by the instructor to get started on the Pilates training program. The commission pay system rewards instructors that actively recruit new clients and work with clients to accomplish their goals. Also, if the studio pays a percentage, the system will be fair and even in regards to the amount of money coming in and the amount of money being paid out." Everything seemed clearer to me now.

"Why didn't the schools teach you how to get a job or how to sell?" "The schools are business first and the most important thing for them is to get students to pay the fee for completing the class, when you pay they make money. If the schools focused on selling or the hardships of clients not showing up for their 5am appointments a good percentage of the students would not complete the course. Lets face it, the realities of the business world are not always pleasant."

He went on to say, "Listen I don't have all the answers and being an instructor is not just fun and games. You will have days just like in any job where things will not fall your way. You will have days where you boss will ride you for sales, you will have days where all your clients will flake out, and days where no one will buy what you are selling, you may even have your favorite client tell you that they are in love with you. Be aware that you are dealing with people and be prepared for all the problems that can come with that. My best advice to you is for you to understand that companies need people like you, and you are a very valuable resource. Go to the establishment that you think will be right for you, talk to some of the instructors and find out if the organization fits in with what you are looking for. You must understand that most large companies have put a substantial amount of time into the systems that they trust and use. They are looking for motivated individuals that will learn these systems, perfect them, and then take them to new levels once they have been fully absorbed. Be open to working hard at first and believing in company values, once that has been accomplished you can have your own ideas about how to run a large Pilates studio training department. **Maybe someday you will be writing the courses for the future training classes.**"

After meeting with my friend, I felt that most of what he had said made sense. I certainly felt that after the time and effort I had put into becoming a Pilates instructor, it was not my nature to just give up and throw all that education and hard work down the drain. I decided that it was time for me to confront my fears and find out everything I could about being a Pilates instructor in the real world.

The first thing I wanted to know is why and how Pilates became the business it is today. As far as I could tell from my research, coaching in some form or another had been around since the beginning of organized sports.

He introduced the work to Los Angeles on March 17, 1971

As far as I could tell the founder of the modern Hollywood movement was a man named **Ron Fletcher!** He began life as a boy in Dog town, Missouri and ended up in New York City with Martha Graham and Joe and Clara Pilates as teachers. I think there were higher powers that lead him along a path and that left no room for random chance. He felt that many students are drawn to his work by the same higher power that led him to create special teachers.

He Arrived...

In New York City in 1944 he was able to secure a job in advertising at Saks Fifth Avenue. Shortly after, He attended a dance concert by the Martha Graham Company and he knew that this was where he needed to be. Ignorant of all protocol, he presented himself and persistently waited until he was granted an interview with Martha. She agreed to allow him to study. Looking back, he could see that he had the natural physical gifts that one needs for the rigors of dance. Still his study had commenced late for a dancer. He did not have the luxury of years of basic dance classes that prepare the artist for performance. The Graham technique is very strenuous and he began to have problems with his knee. Exploratory surgery was recommended. However, this was very risky and could have ended his career. One of the fellow classmates suggested that he should take a trip to see **Joe Pilates**. This is how he began the study of Controlling.

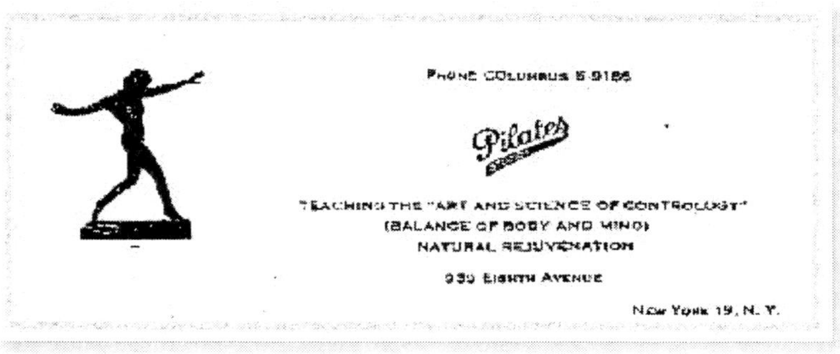

I believe that he was a fortunate person to have been trained on the PILATES REFORMER by Joseph H. Pilates himself, almost 50 years ago, and he clearly recalls how good it felt "The work was constantly evolving and (I'm so grateful) he used me often to try some piece he wanted to see on a body that was beginning to show the Pilates training."

Who in Hollywood doesn't do Pilates these days? It seems you can't flip through a magazine or turn on the TV without hearing someone crediting Pilates exercise with their sleek physique.

The dozen or so TV commercials are packed with testimonials from the rich and famous. Once the best-kept secret of the dance community, Pilates has been discovered and embraced by singers, models, athletes, actors. So it's got to be good for us mere mortals, right?

For what it's worth, here are a few celebrities and sports icons devoted to Pilates exercise.

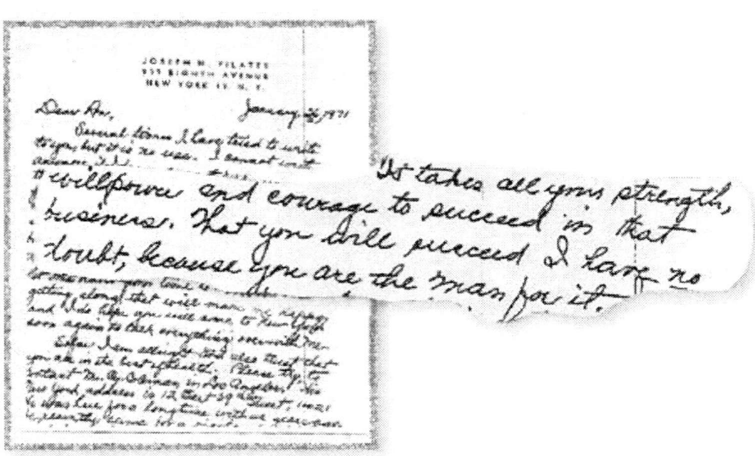

It takes all your strength, willpower and courage to succeed in that business. That you will succeed I have no doubt, because you are the man for it.

He continued working with Martha Graham during this period of time. A student on scholarship, he tread carefully between these two brilliant visionaries (with giant egos) who were both proprietary about their young male students. But I'm telling a big TRUTH when he said he learned a lot – not only extraordinarily beautiful movement, but how to perform it correctly, from deeply within the body, with spirit and with brio, finding a way to understand the philosophies of these two incomparable teachers.

In his early twenties, he went on with his career, working with Martha Graham, dancing on Broadway and in London with Mary Martin, choreographing "Top Banana" with Phil Silvers, choreographing the Ron Fletcher Dancers on NBC's weekly ALL STAR REVUE!

With scant formal education, he was given an honorary degree in 1951 from Utah State University so that he could spend a summer there as resident teacher/choreographer. He also worked with Alma Hawkins in her movement therapy program at UCLA and Santa Monica College with honorary degrees (1975-1977).

He was an Irish/American Indian gay Gemini- a top candidate for alcoholism, and had progressed to the point where he was crazy and impossible to work with when he was drinking, which was most of the time. He began to black out, disappear, smash up bars, and miss rehearsals and openings. Easter Sunday April 15, 1967 was his first AA meeting and from that day he hasn't had a drink for over 37 years.

He did no work for a year, and spent time evaluating, taking inventory of himself, and deciding what he wanted to do!

He continued to maintain his relationship with Clara Pilates through letters and visits to New York.

He introduced the work to Los Angeles on March 17, 1971 and thanks to Aida Grey, Howard Borris and Hal David, he opened a beautiful studio just above Aida Grey's Salon de Beauté, smack on the corner of Rodeo Drive and Wilshire Boulevard in Beverly Hills. As no one outside of Manhattan was familiar with or knowledgeable about the name Pilates, he called his studio The Ron Fletcher Studio for Body Contrology. "Many people in show biz knew my name and "Body Contrology" gave it weight and mystique. I've always liked the term Body Contrology." Joe said "it means discipline: control of the body, mind, breath and spirit." He thanks him...

...this was a new thing for people to discover and try, and talk about. It was in the "right" location and "Ron Fletcher" had done some good work, and was a "real character." Judith Krantz, Ali Macgraw, Candice Bergen, Dyan Cannon, Steven Speilberg, Striesand, Gabor... all came. They recognized it as "good stuff." They liked the change in their bodies, they felt good, they told their friends and they came and the place became an oasis for these people to gather and chat and work and behave like real people.

Jennifer Aniston
Catherine Bell
Pat Cash
Kim Catrall
Kim Coles
Joan Collins
Courtney Cox
Cindy Crawford
Michael Crawford
Jamie Lee Curtis
Susan Dey
Minnie Driver
Daisy Fuentes
Danny Glover
Hugh Grant
Shalom Harlow
Cleveland Indians
Jessica Lange
Lucy Lawless
Madonna
Carrie-Anne Moss
Martina Navratalova
Gwyneth Paltrow
Sarah Jessica Parker
Stefanie Powers
San Francisco 49ers
Martha Stewart
Rod Stewart
Sharon Stone
Patrick Swayze
Uma Therman
Charlize Theron
Tina Turner
Vanessa Williams
Kristi Yamaguchi

That first studio in Beverly Hills became a singular, warm, fine, friendly place to work and teach and learn

BODY CONTROLOGY

The success and popularity of the Beverly Hills Studio and the St. Francis Hospital facility brought in more and more people interested in teaching the work. They came to the studio for lengthy periods of time, learning the basic concepts of the work and serving as apprentice teachers before receiving certifications like the one described above.

The Evolution of the Ron Fletcher Work…

"Joe had always exhorted us to "breathe… you got to OUT de air to IN de air!" However, there was not a clearly shaped breathing pattern for the various moves, and Graham's response to "where and when do he breathe?" was "I don't care as long as it doesn't show." This is the way dancers and athletes work, grabbing a breath when you can. Martha's concept of contraction and release was closing the body and sinking down to the floor on a deep exhalation, and opening the body and filling your "space" on inhalation. Graham often said: "let the inhalation be the inspiration for the movement." It was the coupling of these ideas that influenced the development of my own concept of Percussive Breathing.

I did lengthy research on THE BREATH when I began to write my book. I was astounded after reading the following excerpt: "Each of us is made up of seventy trillion cells and every cell is hungry for oxygen all the time." I observed and experimented more and found, like Joe said, we have to OUT the oxygen-depleted air so that we can IN more oxygen-rich air. So, I began adding structured breathing patterns to the movements… developing what I called **Percussive Breathing**, breath with rhythm and sound... exhaling more completely in order to inhale more fully, expanding the lungs, delivering more oxygen to those 70 trillion cells (from brain to the toenails). My breathing patterns support and bring vitality, exuberance, spirit and enthusiasm to the every piece of movement.

After the publication of my book, with its attendant publicity and television exposure, I was asked more and more to come out to various facilities around the country to conduct workshops. The original

Pilates Work of Joe and Clara had all been done on various pieces of equipment of Joe's design. However, many dance studios with no Pilates equipment, some at university level, asked me to teach "Ron Fletcher Classes" and I began to develop a full curriculum of exercises and movement- standing in place, seated on the floor and moving across the floor that could be done without Pilates equipment.

I made adaptations to the classical pieces of Joe's equipment work, variations on themes, so that this material could be presented on the floor effectively, and I sought to create pieces of movement rather than just a series of exercises. My aim was, and is, to have every piece of vertical body work that is on the floor- seated, standing or moving across the floor, relate to work on the equipment in some way- adding a breath pattern to each piece, stressing both the esthetic and therapeutic aspects of the work-I thought of Clara's admonition, "This machine is your partner," and over a long period of time developed (still am developing) a syllabus of Fletcher Floorwork®, which, to a great degree, can be transferred back to the various pieces of equipment- some including the Fletcher Towelwork®, all of it using the Percussive Breathing patterns. I consistently strive to teach the Pilates concept of working from the low pelvic area "bolting" the pubic bone back to the tailbone, "centering" the body, getting all of its parts into correct alignment, from the foot centers to the top of the back of the head. I used as inspiration for floor work, exercises such as the hundreds (the abdominals), the mermaid, the dolphin, coordination, the elephant and the teaser.

My background as a Graham dancer helped me to develop this material for a floor class that did not depart from the intention of Joe's reformer material. The artistry of the Graham work also influenced my performance and interpretation of the work. I was greatly impressed with Martha's original concept of contraction and release work. This expanded my awareness of the articulation of the spine emphasized by Joe throughout his program. Joe Pilates was adamant regarding his concept of how the body should be placed in an elongated position on the floor. I adapted my roll down series on the floor with the legs in the diamond position from Joe's work on the ped-i-pul. Furthermore, my adaptations on the Spine Corrector gave us the increased abdominal strength and centering in the trunk muscles necessary to perform these new variations of Joe's exercises correctly. I took this awareness with me into the deep contraction and high release of the Graham work, and over time these elements became woven together into a body of work that would challenge and fulfill the workshop students, and have value as a total movement experience.

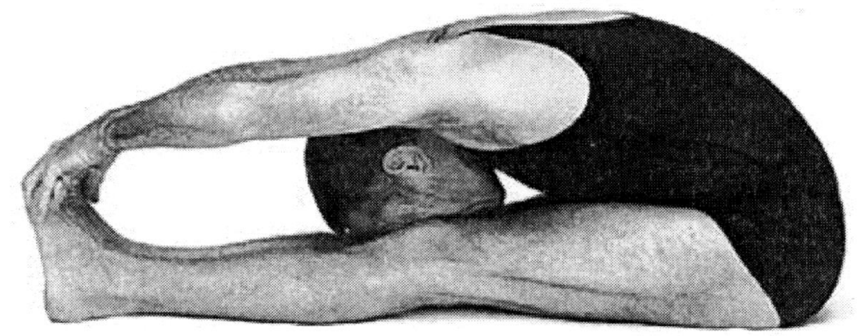

Many instructors of the Pilates work protested vehemently: "Ron Fletcher does not teach classic Pilates, don't study with him etcetera..." I was irritated and bored with all of the litigation going on about who could teach Pilates, who could use the name, and who could not. The quality of work was diminishing as more and more unqualified instructors paid their way into the field in order to cash in on this hot new "old" exercise regimen. I pulled away from using the name Pilates, because first, I wanted to avoid being associated with all the unqualified people out there claiming to be Pilates Teachers. Secondly, I didn't want my teachers, or me to be harassed and possibly sued by a zany person claiming to have the "rights" to everything connected with the name Pilates.

Consequently I obtained a trademark for The Ron Fletcher Work® in 1993 and put together a movement regimen strongly based on my early work with Joe, using Pilates equipment, my high-level, detailed study with Clara, paying heed to her wisdom and depth of knowledge of how and why the work "worked." I brought in much of what I had learned from Martha Graham, Yeichi Nimura, and Alma Hawkins. All of these people were brilliant visionaries.

They all presented movement that was true, organic and therapeutically "right." They simply packaged their products differently. Soon many of Hollywood's elite actors and actresses were using this newfound system for getting optimal results in a Pilates studio."

Soon everyone in Hollywood was talking about experiencing incredible success with the help of his or her Pilates instructor. Hollywood stars could afford to have a Pilates instructor, but it would take some time and a considerable amount of effort to convince the average working class citizens to spend their hard earned dollars on one-on-one sessions.

My first experience in the world of selling fitness came from working in a large Pilates studio chain as a Pilates counselor although I was more interested in being an instructor at the time and had been involved in sports just about every waking day of my life. At that time selling Pilates was the position they had open so I took it, anything to get your foot in the door. Pilates selling was just starting to become something of an art form. Something that only a very few incredibly skilled and highly trained individuals were able to do well. At the time, there were only a couple of companies that had more than ten or so studios. Systems had not yet been standardized and most Pilates studio chains had just recently started to develop a culture that could produce any substantial profits. This was the era that Pilates studios went from business to big business!

Before that, owning a studio was really only for people who wanted to do Pilates and did not care about offering quality equipment or services, this suicidal proprietor could never dream of producing a living. During this time, most Pilates studios only sold a couple of items such as t-shirts and sessions. Pilates was something that was very rare, used mainly in a rehab situation or by some incredibly rich starlet. The Pilates studio business had gone through a sort of metamorphous in regard to the fact that they had discovered EFT. This was a huge breakthrough that created a re-occurring long-term income from a business that had a hard time collecting payment. It was also a time when investors started to see the light on the possibilities of taking a small business and turning it into an anchor institution that would be needed by the average American. This was also the time when the computer became the norm in the average business or household. For the first time people had discovered how to do away with most of the manual labor that had been commonplace in keeping people fit. To be honest, the computer industry was the main factor for the increasing obesity of the average American.

As the Pilates studio industry experienced a huge increase in usage, it became evident that people were beginning to realize that this was something that was growing into a necessity. As the business grew, it also matured into well defined and incredibly effective sales and marketing systems. As these systems were put into place, they were tested, tried, and improved by the people in the trenches, the gifted individuals who had spent many years developing a system that could work in a Pilates studio. These systems were developed from a business that had everything going against it and was still able to create an income. Selling Pilates is unlike any other retail product. You have to think of the customer as an addict. This is the thing that most individuals don't understand about the business.

When a person wants something, they go out and they buy it. When a person wants to change their lifestyle, they will never do it unless someone helps them, the reason most addicts never recover is because they don't have the willpower to do it on their own. Poor lifestyle addicts are begging for relief, but they are not going to ask you to take away their best friend (poor lifestyle). I mean think about it, what person wants to change from pizza and beer, to chicken and rice and when asked that question, how many people are going to say yes to it right now?

The systems that I have used and embraced are the most successful ones that I have ever seen. I have been an open minded student of the business of fitness for over 12 years. In markets all over the world and in studios from small to large I searched for the most successful way to make selling Pilates an enjoyable experience for every person who steps foot through the door of a Pilates studio/center, from the front desk person to the owner, from the client to the instructor these words and systems are gold!

Chapter 21

THE WAY TO MAKE YOUR POTENTIAL CLIENTS KNOW THAT THEY DON'T KNOW

You stimulate their thought process through a series of questions, and must remember to let the guest answer each question fully and completely before asking your next question. There is an old saying that goes, "telling is not selling."

One of most common objections that you may encounter will come in varying forms. It is important to eliminate this problem before it stops you from closing a sale. In order to devise a plan of action for your clients you must first get them to understand that they need your help. This is best done on the floor as the last place you want hear "I want to try it on my own," is at the table when trying to close the deal. Develop a plan of action that will make your client understand that they need your help; do this in a manner that is consistent with your approach prior to the sales process. The most important aspect of helping the guest come to a conscious realization is not an easy task. There are several steps that the client must go through in their minds in order to be fully aware that they don't know what they thought they knew.

1. The first step is the unconscious incompetence, that's where your client isn't aware of what they don't know.

2. Step number two is the conscious incompetence, that's where your client realizes what they don't know.
3. Step three is the conscious competence, that's where they have to think about it in detail before they are able to complete a set task.
4. Step number four is the unconscious competence, that's where an individual is able to perform a task with great ease and without having to think about it.

Knowing these steps to the human behavioral learning process you will begin to understand and pre-determine a set path for preparing your client's mind. I have developed a system that I use for preparing the member to understand that they need my help. The system consists of a three-step process.

I use this three-step system in all of my clubs. It would be difficult for a guest to not know the answers to all of these questions and still say they do not need any help.

Step 1: A statement of fact: "*We have 50 reformers. They are used for muscle toning and strength conditioning. They are state of the art and have springs and boards to protect your joints from injury. They also help one establish torso stability and postural alignment while working limbs in a wide range of motions. Adjustable high quality springs allow for progressive resistance, which helps to lengthen and strengthen the muscles rather than building bulk. It makes for an effective, no-impact stretching and toning workout that is friendly to the joints.*"

Step 2: The above is followed by two to three questions that will enable the potential client to understand that we have information that can help them to be more successful, and to accomplish their goals faster than they would working out on their own. "*Mary, do you know what your target heart rate is?*" "*Mary, are you aware of the exact time, intensity, and duration that you should spend on the* Rock Maple Studio Reformer *for optimal results?*"

Step 3: Step three is a tie down. A tie down is a question that invokes a "yes" response or gains agreement from the client. To help me accomplish this, I simply nod my head when I use a tie down. *"Mary, it sounds like you may benefit from having one of our certified professionals tell you about how to establish torso stability and postural alignment while working limbs in a wide range of motions."*

I use this three-step system to describe several areas of the Pilates studio equipment or my studio. It would be difficult for a potential client to not know the answers to all of these questions and still say they do not need any help. Also remember that some small talk and rapport building is important during your orientation. You do not want to sound like you know it all. Telling your potential client that they need to lose weight or they need to get in shape will just invoke thoughts of doubt. I have found the art of selling Pilates is based mainly on asking questions to help our guests think for themselves and make their own decisions. You stimulate their thought process through a series of questions and must remember to let the guest answer each question fully and completely before asking your next question.

There is an old saying that goes, "telling is not selling." Wouldn't you agree? If you tell someone they need to tone their muscles or need to get started on a Pilate's program, they may believe you or they may doubt it. If you ask a person what brought them in today, and they say they need to tone and improve flexibility, in that person's mind, it is true. The question, "What brought you in today?" stimulates people to ask themselves, "Why *did* I come to the studio today?" After they answer your question, you may even want to follow up by asking, "Why do you want to tone and improve flexibility?" They may answer, "My doctor told me I had to get fit," or, "My clothes do not fit me anymore." At this point you may follow up that question by saying, "How does that make you feel?" These different questions will stimulate the guests to think on their own. It is important to let the guests make their own decisions based on their own thoughts. These thoughts can be stimulated through questions, not by statements and not by you telling them.

I have listed some questions that you can ask and the areas in which you can ask them, as well as some great tie downs to make your tours more effective. There are many ways to give a tour, and this is just one of them. It gives you room to add your own style whereby you should try to create excitement and awe wherever possible.

Proper Food Intake

Questions

1. 1. How important would you guess that proper food intake is for you to accomplish your Pilates goals?
2. 2. How is your food intake right now?
3. 3. Did you know that "hunger" is actually the biggest enemy to accomplishing body fat reduction?

Tie Downs

1. 1. Proper food intake is actually 40 to 50 percent of your success, so can you see the importance of meeting with Mary to have a meal plan strategy customized according to your lifestyle and food preferences, correct?
2. 2. Can you see how meeting with Mary will eliminate all of your guesswork related to food intake and accomplishing your goals? That is something you are definitely interested in, right?

Proper Flexibility and Strength Prescription

Questions

1. 1. Are you aware of what your proper spinal alignment is? Do you know why it is important?
2. 2. Are you familiar with the Frequency, Intensity, Time, and Type (FITT) principle?

3. Do you have a complete understanding of how one establishes torso stability and postural alignment while working limbs in a wide range of motion.

Tie Downs

1. 1. How would you like to have an instructor show you the least amount of reformer training necessary to accomplish your goals?
2. 2. Isn't it nice that we have instructors to eliminate your guesswork and design the most effective program for you?

Proper Supplementation

Questions

1. 1. Did you know that if you are exercising and you are not supplementing, your metabolism is probably not functioning optimally?
2. 2. Did you know that it is well documented that if you were to get all of the nutrients your body needs to truly be functioning at its best from food alone that you would have to eat more than 4,500 calories a day? How close do you think you would get to your goal of eating 4,500 calories a day?

Tie Downs

1. 1. There are a lot of products here that do a lot of different things. Fortunately you do not need to take all of them, right? And even more fortunate, isn't it nice to have a fitness professional that will educate you so you do not have to figure it out all by yourself?
2. 2. Aren't you glad that you can work with a fitness professional to eliminate all of your guesswork when it comes to supplementation?

Proper Resistance Training

Questions

1. 1. Are you aware of why resistance training is important for someone with your goals of reducing body fat?
2. 2. Do you know the difference between resistance training with reformer or without a reformer? Do you feel that what you have done in the past has given you the best possible results?

Tie Downs

1. 1. How would you like to work with an instructor and get set up with the ideal number of sets, reps, and rest periods, and which exercises are best for achieving your goals?
2. 2. Does it make sense that if you are going to be completely set up for success you would want to have a certified instructor to personally customize your program to suit your individual needs?

Again, these are just suggestions. Adapt these to your needs and include some questions of your own. These questions and tie downs have been tried and tested for many years and have been met with outstanding results.

Chapter 22

TIME MANAGEMENT

Part of the reason why I have been successful managing sale systems is I have always kept the systems simple, and I avoid using a computer. We are in a people business

Effective time management is imperative in order to lead a successful life. Everyone from students, to housewives, to the CEO must have a structured system that creates good habits. I cannot stress enough the impact effective proper time management can have on your success in life. You only have so much time and when that time is up, your life is over. For many of us procrastination takes over, bad habits are formed and we never accomplish the things we want in life because we do not have good time management skills.

One of the owners that I used to work for was always quick to bring up a story about his ditch digging theory. He would say that one of his employees would spend all day digging a ditch. It was deep, long and faultlessly round. It was a perfect ditch. He worked hard all day and he was happy with his accomplishment. When he was finished, he would come back into the club and say, "I worked hard all day. I even have blisters on my hands and now I am finally done. Isn't it a beautiful ditch?" And the owner would reply, "Yes, you have worked hard and indeed it is a beautiful ditch. There is only one problem, we don't need a ditch!"

The story is to remind you that your job is to sell Pilates and get clients results. It is important to keep to the main thing, *the main thing.* Work smart, not hard, and stay focused on the business at hand. If your studio is like mine, you only get paid for selling and completing sessions. Do you realize that if you spend 10 minutes a day saving money, 10 minutes a day learning a foreign language, 10 minutes a day writing a book and 10 minutes a day on building a house that in a couple of years, you would have saved a lot of money, you would speak a foreign language, would have written a book and even built a house all in under 40 minutes a day. I relate time management to the prospective client sitting across from you during a sale. Every day you know you should do these things, but every day your mind tricks your body into "thinking about it," trying it out, into putting it off until the next day. That "other day" will never come. You will be an old person sitting around telling yourself, "I should have, I could have, if only…" My mentor taught me one of the most valuable lessons I have ever learned in this business. He said to me, "Have a five-year plan, have a one-year plan, have a monthly plan and have a daily plan." Looking back on this advice now, I did not always hit my daily plan. But I came pretty close. I did not always hit my monthly plan, but I came pretty close. I did not always hit my annual plan, but I would come pretty close. I think you know the answer to the five-year plan. Achieving small goals is the foundation for reaching the large ones. Take baby steps. No step is too small, and no goal or dream is too big. If you have a plan and manage your time then your dream can be accomplished.

My whole system is based on accountability and time management. The system can only work if you use it, and you can only use it if you manage your time correctly. Sit down with your manager or mentor and put together your goals. Once you have done that, work toward devising a plan in order to achieve those goals. In the end, anything can be achieved.

What I Should Do When I Get to Work

1. Walk through the studio. (Meet and greet clients and check equipment for maintenance and cleanliness.)
2. Confirm Pilates appointments and orientations.
3. Update your statistics and personal planner.
4. Update and check the Master Training Appointment Book.
5. Check and call all new clients agreements from the previous day and make orientation appointments and use welcome greetings.
6. Schedule at least three orientation appointments.
7. Sit in on three new clients presentations.
8. Workout with one other Pilates instructor and compare techniques, role-play on sales presentations.
9. Check-out with your Pilates supervisor and make sure your goals are achieved.

Chapter 23

PILATES TRAINING RE-SIGNS

The sales job is about opportunities. The more opportunities you have the more sales you can make! Lost and untracked opportunities are the acts of a fool.

Re-signing a Pilates client can be just as important as signing a new one. Not only is it important in helping your clients to accomplish their goals, but also crucial in maintaining a steady income. Many of the successful instructors that have had long-term success do so through a steady and reliable source of re-signing clients. It is important to remember that many Pilates enthusiasts prefer to do Pilates only when they have a Pilates instructor present. Developing a consistent system for re-signing clients will ensure a quality recurring Pilates business.

Having good long-term success as a Pilates instructor can be very rewarding. This can only happen if you are able to maintain a healthy relationship with your occupation. You should get along with your clients, that is, if you're forced to train people that you are not comfortable with, you may find that your job is intolerable. Loving what you do, or dreading the mere fact of even showing up to work, could all depend on picking and choosing a quality group of clients that you yourself feel comfortable with.

Once you have established a quality group of clients, you may then begin to determine your hours, your number of clients, and even the rates you charge. These benefits may only be enjoyed if you are able to maintain and re-sign a quality client list.

I will give you several presentations that will help in your ability to re-sign a quality client list.

"Mary, I couldn't help but notice that you only have 3 sessions of Pilates left. I'm also sure that you are aware that tomorrow is the final day for our closeout special. We have had incredible success together and I think you would agree that we want to continue in accomplishing all of our original goals. Your success is my success. I would recommend that you reserve your 8:30 time slot before one of my other clients tries to take it."

A Pilates instructor has the unique ability to work with their clients on a daily basis, sometimes using a take-away close can help to set your self up for future success.

"Mary, I know that this may be an uncomfortable question, and I know that you like to start your Pilates sessions after you get off work at 6pm. I have a VIP client who is interested in taking sessions and retaining my services. If you are not interested in re-signing on a long-term package, I may have to reserve this time slot for another individual."

As you begin to evolve as a Pilates instructor and as a sales person you will start to realize that the two things are not separate, they are one in the same. In the beginning, it is important to focus on each separate area, but as you become more experienced, you may start to realize that selling is part of the job. My Pilates re-sign presentation has evolved so far that I don't even give my clients an option.

"Mary, as my client, you agreed that you would put a 100% effort in accomplishing your goal. As your Pilates instructor, I feel that it is my job to give you no other option than accomplishing your original goal. I have already filled out your agreement for another 20 sessions, this was a special package price that our studio offered, and I told my boss to reserve 20 sessions at the discounted rate. Mary, do you want to handle your package by cash or credit card."

It is impossible to get your clients results if you cannot get them to complete their Pilates training. The most important thing to remember in re-signing your clients is that you cannot wait until they finish their entire package, if you wait till the last session, you will have little success in re-signing. You should start selling Pilates when your client has 3-4 sessions left.

Chapter 24

MASTER APPOINTMENT BOOK

The master appointment book (MAB) is an important tool used in health clubs and most service businesses. This important tool is the foundation for team production. If preparation is the key, then this book is the key to success. I believe it would be difficult to fail as a sales manager if you master the art of keeping your MAB filled with quality appointments and follow up on those appointments.

When I use the master appointment book, I make 30 sheets for the whole month and put the names of each salesperson on the top of each page. Each separate sheet should have the times and an area next to them for their names and telephone numbers. There should also be an area for the results. The reason we use the MAB is to track all of the leads and sales in the health club. Then, through practice and repetition, we learn how to most effectively turn these valuable appointments into revenue. Be sure to track all of your individual appointments for the month, closeouts, and for the next day. You should write your appointments in the master appointment book right when you book them, or call up to the front desk and have them written in for you. Daily goals can also be recorded in this book. Remember to take notes and get more than one telephone number.

Let's say YOU take a telephone inquiry. Once you have booked an appointment you call the front desk to let them know. Make sure they write down the telephone number and the appointment date on the TI sheet. Then you write the appointment down in the master appointment book for the time and day that it is scheduled. Include the name, work/home number and cell telephone number if possible. Your planner or personal appointment book should be your master plan for the month. There should be no appointments in any planners that are not also in the master appointment book.

The master appointment book also gives you a list of people to call, such as no-shows, missed sales, and so on. The first job given to a salesperson moving into a management role is to manage the master appointment book. The reason for this is obvious. If you can manage the master appointment book, you are managing the first step of production. *The rule for appointments is half show, half join. So if you have 10 appointments a day, 5 will show and 2.5 people will join.* Two point five memberships per day will make you a successful salesperson. A good fitness manager knows how to run and drive appointments. The master appointment book should be checked several times a day to ensure it is being utilized correctly and consistently. It is a tool that can be used to monitor the progress of the health club as well as keep an eye on how the club is set up for future dates. "John, you have no appointments for tomorrow and only two appointments for closeout, and close out is in three days." If you find that you are deficient in a specific area when it comes to appointments, you can have an appointment marathon. For instance, you can have salespeople coming into the telephone room for one hour and whoever makes the most appointments in that hour gets a free lunch or a cash bonus. You can have every salesperson make one appointment per hour.

For example: coming into the office at exactly twelve o'clock, everyone gets on a telephone and as soon as they book one appointment they are done. You will do that again at one o'clock and again at two o'clock. Each salesperson has to have at least four appointments a day. If you have 10 sales people that will be 10 guaranteed memberships without a walk-in. If you neglect your master appointment book, your sales and production will be greatly lowered.

Production Meetings

The most productive operators in the business know how to HANDLE all the issues in one meeting; this will free up the rest of the day for the important things like grossing.

The MAB should be checked for appointments everyday during the production meeting in order to set goals for the day, regardless the goals for previous day were hit or not. This is also the perfect time to do so because during the production meeting all sales counselors should be in attendance with their planners completely filled out. Anything that needs to be added to the MAB can be added at that time.

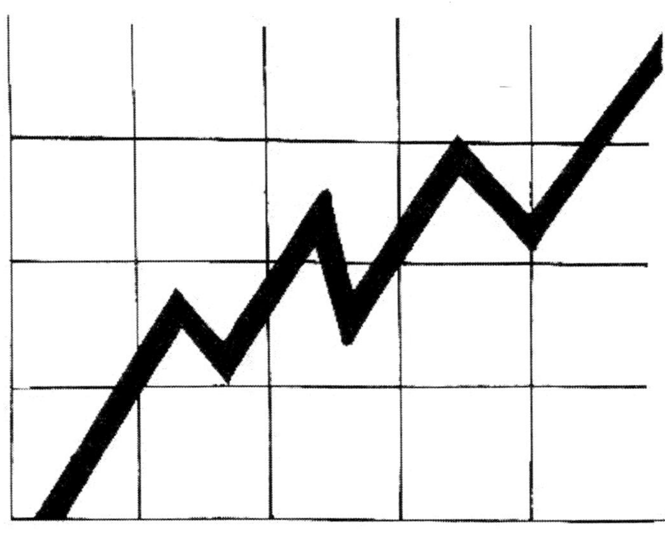

Chapter 25

WORKING THE FLOOR

I don't know if you are as lucky as I am. I have the great fortune of working in a Pialtes studio that is located inside of a large health club. The beauty of working in a Pilates studio can come from many different aspects in our business. If you are selling anything from cars to copy machines to Pilates, the hardest thing about the job is getting the people in front of you. When I refer to the beauty of our business, I am referring to the fact there is a steady stream of customers flowing into our facility at any given moment. I see many Pilates instructors, who think that the only way to make a living is to wait for walk-ins or wait for their orientation appointments to show up. The truth of the matter is evident that all the business you will ever need to make a substantial income is right in front of your eyes. If you have ever worked in a studio that does very little advertising or has very little walk in traffic you would have had to rely on other avenues to create your income. There are some very simple rules that can make a difference in your ability to work the floor. Follow these rules and you will never have to worry about walk-ins or waiting for the guests to come to you.

You must offer Pilates sitting down. I cannot give you a detailed explanation of why it is important to present Pilates sitting down. But your odds of closing a sale increase substantially once you are sitting at the table.

Rule 1:

For the majority of the clients that are working out in your particular facility image is everything. Most of our clients will not admit that they need help. It is important to understand that your clients may not understand how to get results or even how to do basic Pilates. This absence of knowledge may create shortcomings in your clients' abilities to get results, as most clients will not ask for help. You must understand that this gap exists.

Rule 2:

Although it is important to contact your clients, it is also very important to make sure you are not intrusive. One common complaint that I hear from clients that work out in a Pilates studio, is that they feel the instructors tend to be overly aggressive. When I approach a client on the floor, I never linger. I may say something like "I noticed your technique and I though I might be able to offer some pointers. My desk is right over here. And if you like, stop by to see me."

Rule 3:

This rule has made a substantial increase in my ability to add creditability to my knowledge. I have a detailed filing system of articles that pertain to all aspects of health and Pilates. These articles may vary from a wide range of different topics on anything from medical conditions, to how to do Pilates properly. I have articles from supplementation to injury rehabilitation. It is important in any type of sale to give before you get. I may offer to make copies of the article for the member, the web sites for studio business or Pilates management magazines which offer years of back issues and have detailed articles for the purpose of education.

Rule 4:

It is important to remember that you can offer a quick session. This would include going out and using one of the reformers to do some basic exercise, offering a short session for no cost. The best time to go out on the studio floor and offer some pointers would be NOW! Don't be afraid or hesitate when it comes to taking your client through a quick Pilates run thru based on education, giving your clients the service that they came to a Pilates Studio for.

Rule 5:

Although most instructors spend a substantial amount of time on education and on the exercise knowledge, most instructors will fall short when it comes to producing an income. Asking for money is part of being a Pilates instructor. If you cannot get a client to enroll into a Pilates package, you will have very little success in helping your clients get results. It is important to practice the use of high quality presentations such as those mentioned in previous chapters, that have been tested and tried and have been proven to be successful. You should have your presentations memorized word for word and you cannot be afraid of offering your service for a fee. Most of the problems caused in regards to the selling process come from the guest feeling pressured from an untrained, unprofessional instructor using a broken selling system. The instructor may be feeling the same pressure from not memorizing this kind presentation, thus not being prepared. Practice makes perfect!

Rule 6:

You must offer Pilates sitting down. I cannot give you a detailed explanation of why it is important to present Pilates sitting down. But your odds of closing a sale increase substantially once you are sitting at the table.

Rule 7:

The last and most important step that many Pilates instructors fail to adhere to is the good old fashion art of asking for a T/O (take over). Don't be afraid to ask for help. You may just learn something!

Working the floor for Pilates can be a rewarding avenue for a higher income and increasing your client base. This endless source of people can be tapped into if you practice the steps that I have outlined above. Remember as a quality instructor you must have the ability to recruit and keep quality clients, selling is part of your job!

Chapter 26

THE WALL OF FAME

I never hit a shot, not even in practice, without having a very sharp, in-focus picture of it in my head. First I see the ball where I want it to finish, nice and white and sitting up high on the bright green grass. Then the scene quickly changes, and I see the ball going there: its path, trajectory and shape, even its behaviour on landing. Then there is a sort of fade-out, and the next scene shows me making the kind of swing that will turn the previous images into reality. - Jack Nicklaus

I am sure that if you have spent enough time getting to this point in the book, then you are probably like me. You are one of those individuals who spends a substantial amount of time on developing your education level. A good percentage of your time is probably spent studying written material, magazines or articles, or just plain learning from other successful companies in our industry. One of the most successful authors in terms of fitness and their impact on the health and wellness business would be Bill Phillips of EAS. He developed the book "Body for Life." This incredible wellness improvement system was on the New York Times bestseller list for more than a year. Another company that has been extremely successful in terms of their sales and production is Weight Watchers. As students dedicated to improving our ability to recruit, sell and get results for Pilates clients, we have found that one thing these two companies use in a very successful manner would be the before and after concept. This successful concept was used everywhere in the 70s and 80s but seemed to die out during the 90s. Now if you look at these types of sales or marketing techniques, you can see that many companies are going back to this proven success method for promoting their product. In my studios I set up a wall of fame. The wall should have lots of pictures; they should be before and after shots. With today's digital cameras this should be a cinch. The next step is the testimonial. This should come in the form of a letter and, the clients should write it. It should outline the steps that were taken in order to gain success with the Pilates training program.

- **What package did they buy?** This is important because it gives the potential client some insight into what needs to be done in terms of investment and may relieve some of the anxiety about what package to get started on!
- **How many times a week did they work with the instructor?** Working with an instructor requires a bit of re-allocation and life style adjustment. The wall may relieve some of those concerns as well. It may also give your potential client expectations of commitment
- **How long were the workouts and what did they consist of?** The workout routine is very important because seeing the progress and the routine helps the clients see the amount of time and planning that goes into the sometimes complex art of getting your clients results
- **What supplements did they take and what was the food intake like?** Supplements and meal replacements have become commonplace in most training programs and if they are not adjusted properly the results may be slow coming.
- **How many days off did you have?** This will be vital to many of your clients and the days off may be a necessity. Make sure to show that all of your clients may have had a day or even weeks off at some point in the quest for success and these set backs don't stop success. This shows the reality of the program and highlights your compassion to your guests.
- **What was the role of the instructor?** This is the most important part of the wall of fame. You have to explain the role of the instructor and how the instructor made a difference in

the success of the program. For example, Mary stated that she had tried many different programs and this was the first time she had any type of long term success, therefore the instructor was the difference.

- **When did you first start to see results?** For many new Pilates clients the first sign of change is very slow and sometimes weight loss may take two or three weeks before any substantial changes occur. Again it is important to show new clients that they are not alone in this battle and that the successful clients had the same slow start. This is just part of the battle and if others have done it so can they.
- **Show the before and after measurements?** Show the numbers. This is concrete evidence of individual achievements. If you do a good job on the orientation you should have an outline of the before measurements, the body fat percentage, weight, and so on If it is in black and white your clients can visualize their progress and feel proud.
- **And be sure to include the obvious, how do you feel now?** It is also good to let the guests know that once goals have been reached with the assistance of a Pilates instructor one experiences physical rewards. This is important. The feeling of success is something everyone can relate to and should be instilled with a plaque on the wall of fame.

The wall of fame should be put in a high profile place near the Pilates area and should be updated often. The message should be perfectly clear; if you want to be successful you should do what every one else is doing! If you want to be successful; get a Pilates instructor!

Chapter 27

THE CLOSEOUT MASTER PLAN

Someone once told me the atmosphere at the front desk should be like Disneyland. Overly friendly!

As the ultimate Pilates instructor, it is important to use all of the resources possible to develop and enhance your ability to recruit and involve clients in the program. The closeout master plan is a detailed outline of what it would take for you to develop an incredible buying frenzy. In this day and age, most Pilates studios are familiar with a closeout party but there are still many studios that do not believe in having this type of promotional event. In the twelve years that I have worked in the Pilates studio business, I have never seen a studio use a properly developed closeout system and not produce a positive response from the clients, employees and guests. As a Pilates instructor this is a checklist of sorts that you should have in your daily planner. You can go over it starting a couple days before the closeout party to make sure you are successful. One good closeout should represent about five days worth of revenue. One bad closeout is equal to five bad days. Be aware of this and make sure that you are set up and ready. Remember, Pilates studios are about energy. The best operators are the ones that can create the energy, not only among the clients and guests, but also among the staff. The most successful day in retail store sales for many years was a closeout created by Macy's Department Store. "Macy's white flower day," if you can tell me what a white flower day is, you are smarter than me. It has nothing to do with anything other than a sale and the energy created by it.

A closeout in short is a party! A huge fiesta put together to create a buying frenzy. Most Pilates studios will do the majority of the work for you and in mentioning work I am referring to the little things done by your studio that build up the hype. It is still important to understand the process and do your part. All of the studio passes (three and ten days) will expire or be extended on that day. All corporate open enrollment periods should be expiring that day. All special pricing will be expiring that day. One hundred "hot colored signs will be up in the studio, announcements are being made every 10 minutes, the telephone is answered in a different way and all schedules are cleared of client problems, Pilates sessions or nutrition sessions. Closeout is set up for selling only. Post-dated checks or credit cards should all be made for the 15th or the 30th of the month; this creates excitement among the staff. The contest box for the trip give-a-way should be front and center: The most important part about the trip give-a-way or the raffle is that you must be present to win. Also think about making a rule "bringing in a non-client is the only way to enter." The two most important elements of the party are the "raffle" in the evening or throughout the day and having several "outside vendors" coming in to promote their product. This will create a festive atmosphere in your studio. Make sure that all staff members are at the studio by 8:00 a.m. and that the studio is decorated by 9:00 a.m. Make sure to have one person scheduled to come in extremely early because there is a whole group of clients and guests that like to come in early and you may miss an opportunity. You may be able to upgrade a package option or sell some Pilates sessions. The person that wants to make the biggest paycheck is probably the person that will be there early.

The Set Up

1. As you can see from the things I have listed above, the closeout set up starts from the beginning of the month. Developing good habits will ensure your success by following the points outlined above on a daily basis. The most important aspect of your personal performance on closeout will come from your ability to clear your schedule and book only handpicked orientation or sales opportunities. I like to hand pick my closeout orientations and I do this by having a free Pilates try-out booth set up a couple of days prior to the party. I hand pick guests that seem interested. If they seem like they are interested in a Pilates session, I book them for an appointment during our closeout party.
2. Each Pilates instructor or Pilates counselor should have a job assignment for the party. An example would be puttin an instructor in charge of setting up and running a supplement booth. Someone else may be in charge of making sure the studio is decorated with balloons. Another example would be to have one instructor in charge of enrolling vendors to make the event more festive. The key to success will come from your team working from a plan.
3. Each instructor should have approximately 15 orientations set. Those appointments should consist of 30 minute time periods and a goal for production should be set. These appointments should be confirmed and the confirmation call should include a brief explanation outlining the day's events.
4. Each instructor should call 50 current clients and 50 missed guests to promote the closeout party. Call and leave messages and tell your guests and clients about the opportunities, giveaways or even invite them to bring friends and families to workout free of charge.
5. Signs must be up and the instructors, counselors, the front desk staff and even the janitors should know the promotion.

Have it planned and be sure to send out several confirmation calls. Have a production with the staff or be involved in one so that every individual in the company is aware of the promotion and what the signs mean.

6. All "balance dues" and "promise to pays" must be collected or scheduled for closeout. Everyone that owes money should be called and told to come in on closeout to pay their balance or they will be sent to collections.
7. Advise the front desk of telephone salutations and start it today. "Thank you for calling ________________on our closeout sale, how may I help you?" Promote whatever the special is when giving the telephone salutation and attach a copy of it to the telephone.
8. One instructor should be working the front desk all day for "flips" and renewals. Make sure that one person is at the desk working check-ins and making sure that every person that walks in is told about the specials. This is a huge source of revenue for the company.
9. Before Pilates instructors go home make sure that all appointments are written in the master appointment book.
10. All post dates should be put on the books and make sure to write them down the night before closeout. This way you know exactly how much needs to be made in order to hit your goal.
11. Spread the hype with each and every employee about the big day that is happening tomorrow. Make sure that everyone knows and understands what closeout is.
12. The front desk should have a retail or sidewalk sale set up and they should handle any food, fashion shows or sidewalk sales. Managers/supervisors should be doing orientations, potential sales only and be in charge of supplement or Pilates seminars in the fitness room. Nutritionists should clear their schedules and be in charge of vitamin seminars or nutrition seminars. Pilates instructors should do a dance seminar at

some point in the evening or a movement demonstration out in front of the studio.

13. Closeout should not cost the company money and should be part of the employee's job description. The staff will be getting paid extra commission based on the extra sales made. All trips, food and vendors should be traded out with the approval of the general manager or regional manager. No trade outs can be accepted for personal or staff use.

On the Day of Closeout

On the day of closeout you should have this list posted in your office and in your planner and you should make sure to do everything on the list.

1. On closeout, have a morning production meeting and motivate everybody. Get them excited. Let everyone know what is riding on the studios performance by highlighting where the studio is at and what needs to be done in order to hit your goals.
2. Get balloons, streamers, and signs up so the studio looks like there is a party going on.
3. Don't deal with any cancellations or customer service issues today. Today is pure production. No negativity is allowed.
4. Do 25 percent off retail and supplements and set up booths for the promotion of this such as, 'buy 2 get the 3rd one free' or 'buy 1 and get the 2nd one for 50 percent off.'
5. Continue to promote the evening over the telephone.
6. No sessions for employees allowed on closeout.
7. Emphasize paid in full options. Every package should offer 1, 3 or 5 sessions free.
8. Make sure you have something to give-a-way to clients. Do trade-outs with businesses to give away in a drawing on closeout. This creates a buying atmosphere.

9. Have an afternoon production meeting.
10. Nobody "walks" on closeout. Call your district manager to approve deals.
11. Dress in a different or new uniform. In my studios I like to have a theme this gives the staff a chance to wear apparel of their choosing that coincides with the theme. Appearance and presence are half the battle.

Chapter 28

SELLING SUPPLEMENTATION

Strength does not come from winning. Your struggles develop your strengths. When you go through hardships and decide not to surrender, that is strength. - Arnold Schwarzenegger

When I first started in the Pilates studio business, most studios had not yet developed a game plan for promoting supplements; in fact in the early 90s many did not offer supplements as part of their retail centers. The art of selling supplements to our clients is something that is still being developed. There are several effective ways to market our pro shop products.

There have been many debates as to whether or not supplements are good for you. Most Pilates studio supplements are not approved by the F.D.A. this means that they are not required to have specific regulations or ingredients. The lack of regulation for these kinds of products can vary drastically, and long-term effects have yet to be determined. It is important when offering these products that you do not tell your clients and guests that they need to take a certain supplement or vitamins. I always try to prescribe supplements in a manner that is consistent with feedback from other people that have used the products. For example, "we have several clients who have taken this product and have seen substantial changes in their bodies during the time they were using this supplement." Pilates studios have come under scrutiny and have had some law suits associated with instructors telling clients that they wouldn't get results if they didn't take a certain vitamin.

Offering supplementation in your retail center can vary in volume from studio to studio. One studio may sell one jug of protein a week whereas another may sell one hundred. I have worked in high volume retail studios and selling vitamins will be much easer if you follow a few simple steps

- One of two things must happen! Either the studio should offer the vitamins the instructors are taking, or the instructors are required to take the supplements the studio is selling. You guys can figure out the details, but the bottom line is if the staff is using a certain product, this will make it sensationally more desirable. The rule is to consume and sell the products from your studio.
- Put the product in the consumer's hand. Once the product is in the person's hand they will be more likely to show interest. You may then answer questions as you point to the label.
- Know the current discounts - if you know the current promotions you will have more success and you may entice more of your clients to show interest.
- Know your products or find someone that does.
- Attractive display - move the supplements often and use big signs.
- Offer discounts for employees and if you can, have a credit account or V.I.P. discount card.
- Put up signs on all of the equipment.
- Offer drinks with scoops of supplements if you have a juice bar.
- Supplement tables or seminars.
- Use before and after pictures include the list of supplements for the individuals.
- Set up the body for life Pilates challenge. A before and after E.A.S. style contest. Bill Phillips wrote the supplement guide in the mid 90s and has sold more vitamins because of it than any one I can think of.

- Most important is to know your stuff. If you don't know the latest info on any of the particular items at your studio find somebody that does! Don't play the guessing game!

Following some of these simple guidelines will help you and the other clients of the Pilates team move supplement products.

Chapter 29

INTERACTING WITH STAFF

People are often unreasonable, illogical and self-centered: Forgive them anyway. -Mother Teresa

Staff interaction is an overlooked yet vital aspect of our business. Many Pilates instructors and sales consultants fail to do the groundwork and are unable to interact well with others. Loving your job or dreading the thought of even showing up to work could all depend on how well you work with your surrounding staff. Since we are in a commission driven business, instructors can become competitive. At times they will even cross the line of stealing or "sharking" packages. The way to handle these problems is quickly, privately and usually through your manager or fitness supervisor. Problems that are not handled immediately can fester into much larger problems that can affect the entire studio.

Your manager

Your studio manager or fitness supervisor is the person who has the most to gain from your success in the studio. At this level I can almost guarantee the managers are tied into a piece of everything you sell, they truly have a vested interest in making sure that you are successful. I have found that many instructors, being part time or being scheduled to work hours that do not always coincide with the management, often become alienated from the people that are the true professionals in the studio. Spend as much time as you can in an attempt to find out how these individuals think and what they want. Being in tune with the wants and needs of the person that hands out your pay check will increase your ability to grow and to learn from someone who has a proven track record in the industry. It is also important to understand that whenever there is a problem that concerns a new or important client, the manager is the one who will deal with it. In many cases these clients have had problems or need a new instructor. Since they have usually spent (or spend) a lot of money on training, the manager will only hand out these clients to the instructors that they trust or have a good reputation for understanding the company systems.

The most important relationship you can have will be with your front desk staff, as they are the first contact. They can control your paycheck.

Front desk

One time I was upset because one of my important clients scheduled an early morning appointment on my day off of all things. I canceled a trip to meet with them and drove all the way to the studio early in the morning to find that the front desk person had not written down the message. My client had canceled the appointment many days prior. Being in a bad mood from the early wake up call, I let this individual have it! Things really got ugly at that point and not only did I stop getting my messages but I found that my orientations were all kids with no money and people that had no interest in buying Pilates. What I found is that these people actually recommend instructors to many of the clients. I found that many of the potential clients interested in having a Pilates instructor would first ask the service desk staff which person they felt was the best instructor.

Other instructors

Many of the instructors in the Pilates studio business today have a lot of knowledge on different aspects of exercise. It has been through the relationships that I have built in the business that I have been able to keep my knowledge and skills sharp. I spend 2 hours a week making sure that I squeeze in a Pilates practice with one of the other instructors. Ask questions, practice with each other, trade clients, do sales role-playing and rely on them as sales professionals. This instructor can answer a question about an area that is their specialty; this resource is at your fingertips. Use it and build a good relationship with your teammates.

Mentor

Not everyone starts off with great instincts when it comes to being an instructor or the related sales process, but whatever abilities people have can be nurtured and developed. My first six months in a role where I was forced to sell Pilates were very difficult. I felt that I was good with people but I did not have much in the way of natural sales ability. The system that I put together is geared towards people like myself: the 99 percent that are not gifted in sales. I feel that anyone can sell a package if they have the determination and ability to learn the system. There was no system when I started; it was just my mentor and I. He showed me his methods, he critiqued my weak points, gave me encouragement, TOed for me, helped me to understand the rules of the game and showed me the correct way to fill out a Pilates agreement.

I owe most of my early success to my mentor. I probably would not have lasted as an instructor if I hadn't had someone like this to help me. What did he gain in return? That is a simple answer. I worked on his team. If he needed to have someone to stay late, or come in early, I was there. If he needed someone to work on Sunday, I was there. When he became a supervisor, I followed him to every studio that he worked in. I followed thru every task he asked down to the smallest detail. When he became a district director, he promoted me to a manager and sent me to any studio that was doing poorly. I followed the system and increased sales in the low studios so that they became the top studios. Our relationship helped our company become more successful, and in turn, we helped each other in becoming more successful. We made more money, because we worked together.

Top Sales Producer

These are the guys you want to get in good with. In most cases the top sales people in the studio have access to the new clients. The people that have just signed up are the best source of new clients. Building a good relationship with the top sales people will put you in an ideal position to pick and choose the orientations that you feel have some interest in training or have some interest in you as their instructor. As you build this symbolic relationship you may even find yourself being brought in to the sales process to T.O. for training or you may ask the help of the sales department for some help closing one of your clients! It is important to send any new sign ups for Pilates to the top sales person that is helping you and you will see a huge improvement in your Pilates schedule.

Increase Your Sales Knowledge

Every morning on the plains of Africa, the lion awakes, and
knows it must outrun the slowest gazelle or it will starve to death.
Every morning on the same plain, the gazelle awakes and
knows it must outrun the fastest lion, or it will be killed."
It does not matter if you are the lion or the gazelle.
When you wake up in the morning, you'd better be running

As the complete professional, you must continue to grow. You must improve your knowledge, your sales skills and your training information. Our business is a rapidly changing one. If you do not continue to grow, you will be left in the dust. The young people just starting in our business are at the top of their game. They are top athletes trained by the latest technology, and they know there is money to be made in our industry. They are hungry. There is a poster above my desk and it says, *"That's why I've busted my butt on the range for hours on end and made changes to get to this point where I'm able to compete at the highest level in major championships. That's where you want to be." -Tiger Woods*

We work in the one of the fastest growing industries in the world. Computerization has changed the amount of energy that we expel at work. By the year 2010, 25 percent of all Americans will be working from their homes. You literally will not even have to get up and walk in order to accomplish your job. The obesity rate is reaching staggering heights and the amount of information available about fitness grows every day. Doctors are getting smarter, nutritionists are getter better, and supplementation has improved. Lets face it; Pilates centers have come a long way from the old strap machine that jiggles your fat away (by the way, there was still one of those in the first studio that I worked).

Commissions

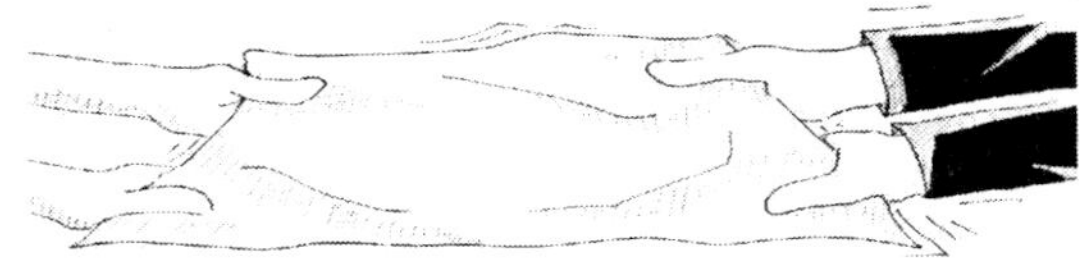

The rules for splits and commissions can be at the forefront of many staff problems that arise in a Pilates studio. It is important to lay down the ground rules for how to handle these sensitive issues. I suggest posting the rules so that every one is clear on how splits and other commissions work.

The interaction between instructors can be a fine line of controversy so the rule that we have used for splits is the following. If an instructor has an appointment, it must be in their planner or in the MAB. If it is not, it is not an appointment. That appointment must be within 24 hours of the day it is written in the book, (same day, day before, day after). If another instructor takes your appointment, it is a split. If you have a potential client come back to the studio, and it is not in the MAB. And they do not ask for you, it is not yours. If a potential client comes into the studio and asks for you, that is your "ask-for" or appointment. If you are with a walk-in, you will receive half. If a potential client on your pass joins the studio, and they don't join with you, and you don't have an appointment, you will get nothing. (You should have closed them when you had the chance.)

Renewals, this part is tricky! The other instructors can only re-sign up a potential client on a Pilates package if; #1 The client has never bought Pilates. #2 The client has a package that has been expired for more than a month. #3 At the point of sale on a new enrollment. Instructors should let all their clients know that if they are interested in any Pilates programs they should go through them and specify that this is how they earn a living. Last but not least, orientations go to the instructor.

These are just some of the rules we run at our studios. We have used these rules for years, and they work very well. Remember, what goes around comes around. If you are not consistent, you will run into problems, in which case remember to handle your issues immediately and fairly. You may even consider posting the rules, so that everybody is clear on them. In one of the studios I worked in, the manager had the sales staff vote on each rule, he then posted the rules on the wall and we never had a problem.

Negativity is the cancer that ruins your paycheck. Do not get caught up in other people's business. Mom always says, "Mind your own business." Remember, if you have complaints or something negative to say, complaints go up. Complaints don't stay level or down, they go up. Keep focused on your business at hand, stay away from the fun bunch and have clear rules of commission. Stay on the good side of all the departments, attend meetings, and follow your to-do list every single day. By following the simple rules of staff interaction, you will truly love your job in the Pilates industry.

Chapter 30

GIVING A FREE GIFT WITH PURCHASE

I don't know why, but the old free gift with purchase gets them every time, just ask the department stores. They have made millions of dollars in their cosmetic departments just by offering a free gift along with a purchase of a package. I have had good success with three different options in reference to a free gift with purchase.

1. The first option that has worked well for our company has also been used to generate interest in almost all of the companies that I have worked for. It is a very simple process, basically if a client enrolls in the starter package, they will receive a limited time prize. For instance, "enroll in the starter package between now and the end of the month and receive a free Sony Walkman. This offer expires 11/30/2004." You can do the same for the accelerated result package. Get started on the accelerated result package between now and the end of the month and receive a free LV wallet. When I use the free gift with purchase program, I only use the item available for about a five-day period and I rarely use the same item twice. Many of these items may be purchased for a discount or a partial trade for free sessions. Remember to ensure your manager has approved all trade outs!
2. The second option has also been used to provide outstanding results and to create urgency at the end of the month. The process for offering the free gift with purchase comes in the form of a larger prize, and depending on the amount

of sessions that you purchase, you will receive one entry for each session. So for example, a client enrolls in the starter package and receives six entries whereas a client that purchases 32 sessions would have 32 entries in the drawing. Once again to create urgency, the drawing is held on close-out and the only people who are invited to participate in this drawing are those who enrolled in the program during the competition dates.

3. The third option is where you have a contest or a challenge that includes a set amount of sessions and a prize for the winner of the challenge. So for instance, the program may require each contestant to complete 32 sessions of Pilates in a 60-day period. Based on the evaluation results taken at the end of the 60-day period prizes can be given to the top three contestants. As an extra incentive you may wish to offer a free T-shirt to anyone who participates.

Avoid giving too much information. Only give information once you have some commitment from your guest.

Chapter 31

CONFIRMING APPOINTMENTS AND CANCELLATIONS

There are three ways you can operate in a Pilates center.
1. You can get setup and get prepared.
2. You can wait for walk-ins.
3. You can pray!

If you have been an instructor for any period of time, you will find yourself in situations where you have the devil on your left shoulder and an angel on your right shoulder. You will be sitting in front of a check with your name on it and a client who is happy to deliver another large package. As you wipe the beads of sweat from your forehead, the words are going through your mind, "Should I or shouldn't I?" Another twenty hours spent in anguish over a client who takes advantage of my generosity and hard work. We talked earlier about the difference between loving your day-to-day life as a career Pilates instructor and dreading the next re-enrollment. It all depends on your ability to keep a healthy relationship with your trade and your client base. Loving your job or dreading the thought of even showing up to work can all depend on how well you establish boundaries with your clients. When it comes to rescheduling and cancellation of appointments, I try to set down the rules for what is and is not acceptable and what it will cost per session. On the following page are some of the rules we run at our studios. We have used these rules for years and they have worked very well for us. If you do not practice consistency it is likely that you will run into problems.

Always remember to handle your issues immediately and consistently. You may even consider posting the rules, so that everybody is clear about them. You can also have your clients sign a waiver that has all the rules listed so that there are no misunderstandings and then post the rules on the wall. We never had problems in the past when doing this as the client is left unable to feign ignorance. The confirmation box will allow you make a note if the appointment has been confirmed. I like to call my appointments from home just to confirm that they are coming in before I leave for the studio. Also, it is important to call and check the book to see if any new appointments have been scheduled for the day. Your clients should have access to your voicemail system so they can call if they have any last minute cancellations.

One of the most important relationships you can have will be with your front desk staff, as they are the first contact. They can control your paycheck.

Agreement for Pilates guidelines

1. All Pilates sessions must be made or rescheduled 24 hours prior to the appointment time. Sessions that are not cancelled in advance may still incur a charge. All clients are responsible for having number of the direct phone line or message center to their particular instructor. Messages left at the front desk or at the corporate office may not reach instructor in time to be considered 24 hour advanced notice.
2. #1 Pilates instructors have hourly Pilates appointments. Please be aware that if you are late, irrespective of your session start time, your instructor must finish on time and not run over.
3. As a #1 Pilates member, you agree to the time limit in which the Pilates package must be completed. If extra time is required to complete the package, this extension must be approved by the #1 Fitness corporate office.
4. All Pilates clients must agree to a physical examination prior to starting a Pilates program. The client is responsible for making sure they are physically fit to exercise.
5. #1 Pilates has agreed to provide an instructor for the sessions indicated. #1 Fitness does not agree to make all of your sessions completed with the same instructor.
6. The client agrees to notify #1 Pilates if at any time they are not comfortable with the Pilates instructor they are working with. Clients may change instructors at any time. The client also agrees to notify #1 Pilates of any extended leave.

Client:____________________ Instructor:____________________

Chapter 32

DRILLING

I never think that there's something I can't do, whether it's beating my opponent one on one, or practicing another hour because something about my game is just not right. - Earvin "Magic" Johnson

Drilling is an essential part of the human behavioral learning process. Repetition is the key to perfection. Every time we do something we get a little better at it and it gradually becomes easier and easier until we reach a point where we can do it without thinking, this is the place that we long to be.

The unconscious competence: You don't have to think about riding a bike, and you don't have to think about catching a ball. You don't have to think about walking. But all of these things at one point in our life were difficult. It took a lot of effort and practice to perfect these simple things. Selling is just as easy as riding a bike, although it may not seem so to a beginner. Most people at the age of five learn to ride a bike. They don't learn to sell. A professional football player practices throwing a football every day of his life and still continues to practice every day once he gets in the pros. All-professional's drill: boxers, basketball players, racecar drivers, doctors and lawyers. Practice, practice, practice, drill, drill, drill.

Mirroring and Matching Drill

This drill requires two Pilates instructors sitting face to face mirroring and matching every movement. You want to focus on the energy, the breathing, everything involved in mimicking the person to a "T".

The Question Game

The question game is a simple but effective way to learn the art of selling. This technique has been instrumental in my ability to train top-notch Pilates sales professionals. Answering a question with a question and staying calm under fire is at the heart of what selling is all about. It took me a long time to develop a drill that could teach the fundamentals that were the real difference between a new sales person and a seasoned one. One day it dawned on me that the difference between a new sales person and a seasoned was as simple as the experienced sales person knowing how to ask questions instead of answering them. This is the little or **big** difference in communication styles! This drill helped put the sales person in control of the conversation thus enabling them to control the thoughts of the guest through a series of questions. When each of the questions is asked the guest needs time to think of the answer and the sales process begins. This drill is my invention and I have never seen it used in any other publication. To perform the drill, sit across from another instructor and ask them a question. The other instructor (in a role playing manner), will then answer with a question, to which you will reply with another question and so forth.

Example:

Pilates Instructor 1: How much does it cost for a Pilates session?

Pilates Instructor 2: Were you looking for a Pilates package for yourself, a family or a couple?

Pilates Instructor 1: Do you have equipment?

Pilates Instructor 2: What kind of equipment are you interested in?

Pilates Instructor 1: Do you have Pilates?

Pilates Instructor 2: Were you interested in a package or a session?

Pilates Instructor 1: What time is the studio the busiest?

Pilates Instructor 2: What time will you be using the studio most?

The Tough Customer Drill

This is a great drill for new instructors that want to become better at selling. You have to learn to be direct and to come back at your guest with the same energy they are giving you. This is not the time to back down. Your potential client is trying to take control, this is their technique. This is the time for you to take control by matching the abrasiveness brought on by the client.

Closing Drill

In a role-playing situation, try to overcome objections given by your studio supervisor or another instructor. Ask your partner, "If I can get you a great deal on a Pilates training package, would you want to get started today?" Have your partner respond by saying, "Not today, maybe, I want to try it first, I would consider it and no." Drill on overcoming these objections. You may try "if it was $10 per session, would you be able to make a decision to get started on the program today?" Also drill on "out of the different package options, which one are you leaning towards?" Your partner would respond with the seven common objections. "I want to think about it!" "I need to speak to my spouse." "It is too much money." Use the steps outlined in overcoming objections. Practice overcoming five objections, and make sure your partner is being realistic: not too hard, and not too easy.

Filling out the Pilates Agreement Drill

This could be one of the most important drills. Most of the Pilates deals that are lost are done so the moment the agreement comes out. Objections start to flow the moment the pen tries to touch the paper. Filling out the contract is the pivotal moment where most new Pilates instructors will lose their potential client or miss their sales. First try practicing by using stalling tactics. Pretend that you are a potential client and try grabbing the Pilates agreement. Practice by answering questions with questions or by tapping your finger at the signature spot. You could try bringing up objections over paying with a credit card and even about payment method or type. You can also mention wanting to return at a later time to pay. If you can master through drilling, the ability to control your potential client during this most important time in the sales process, you will find this will highly increase your closing percentages.

Pilates Presentation

Practice your P.T. presentation until you have learned it word for word. Drill on difficult, detailed questions on fitness that your guest may ask. Your presentation should sound smooth and unrehearsed. You should practice being an empathetic listener and your presentation should leave clients truly understanding the value of the program that you are offering to them. Remember; "practice makes perfect!"

Setting up a Free Session or Orientation

Repetition is the mother of learning and the father of action, which makes it the architect of accomplishment.

When establishing a successful Pilates program, the first step in your success will be filling up your orientation book. Having quality opportunities is the key to any successful business. Drilling on overcoming objections to the free workout is important. You will hear statements such as, "I will try it on my own," or, "I have the Pilates program that my coach wrote up for me in high school." You may even hear, "I don't need an instructor." Overcoming these objections will help you keep your book full and confirm future success.

Mother Teresa of Calcutta Quotes

If you are kind, people may accuse you of selfish, ulterior motives: Be kind anyway.

People are often unreasonable, illogical and self-centered: Forgive them anyway.

If you are successful, you will win some false friends and some true enemies: Succeed anyway.

If you are honest and frank, people may cheat you: Be honest and frank anyway.

What you spend years building, someone may destroy overnight: Build anyway.

If you find serenity and happiness, they may be jealous: Be happy anyway.

The good you do today, people will often forget tomorrow: Do good anyway.

Give the world the best you have, and it may never be enough: Give the world the best you have anyway

You see, in the final analysis, it is all between you and god: It was never between you and them anyway.

Mother Teresa of Calcutta!

Chapter 33

TO SELL OR NOT TO SELL

"To make coaching sessions most productive, hone two essential conversational skills–asking questions and listening to the answers"

To sell or not to sell, that is the question. Recently, we have been hearing the faint whispers of a growing number of business professionals blaming the sales process as the smoking gun for all of the shortcomings in our industry. This negative force has been deemed the reason for some kind of slow growth. When putting some deep thought into this important issue we must look at our industry and we must look into the future as well as into the past. The first question I ask is "**what** slow growth?" The Pilates studio business next to the size of McDonalds or Coke may be the fastest growing thing on the planet. Due to the present downturn in the economy most companies within our core markets failed to survive. While all the other businesses are thinking of ways to improve and enhance the sales process we are thinking of abandoning it.

The shortcomings that we have are a staple in any growing business. Ours come not from the selling process but more from the lack of getting all of our ships to sail in the same direction. Not in the selling process but in the professional level, or lack thereof, which our industry requires for training and keeping a mature staff. Selling is a tool and nothing more "should the chef stop creating his masteries in the kitchen because he is burned by the flame or blame the knife for a nick on the finger?"

Selling is a tool and when used properly it may be referred to as the greatest profession ever created by man! However, it is a very powerful and complicated tool; when used properly it can be extremely effective and when used carelessly it can be dangerous. Studied in depth it is as powerful and infinite as the human mind and yet it is also as basic in human nature as children's first questions. I agree our process must evolve and it will, but it must do so without abandoning the knowledge gained by our predecessors.

We must understand that we are dealing with people as our product. We sell dreams and results and sometimes failure, thus we must endeavor to understand that each and every guest is different. We must also accept that the incredible growth of our industry could be called the most explosive business invention of the century.

To those who say this industry and its systems are not extra ordinary and that growth means the abandonment of competition, victory and selling dreams, I say never.

ISBN 142514742-9

9 781425 147426